COMPLAINT FREE
RELATIONSHIPS

COMPLAINT FREE RELATIONSHIPS

How to Positively Transform Your Personal, Work, and Love Relationships

WILL BOWEN

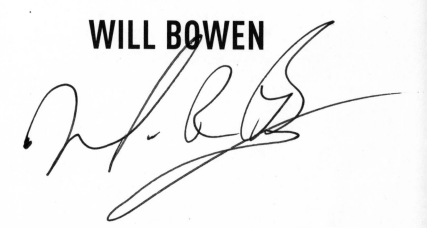

DOUBLEDAY

NEW YORK LONDON TORONTO SYDNEY AUCKLAND

DOUBLEDAY

Library of Congress Cataloging-in-Publication Data
Bowen, Will.
Complaint free relationships : how to positively transform your
personal, work, and love relationships / Will Bowen.—1st ed.
Includes bibliographical references and index.
1. Interpersonal relations. 2. Life skills. I. Title.
HM1111.B69   2009
158.2—dc22   2009036769

ISBN 978-0-385-52975-4

Printed in the United States of America

Design by Meryl Sussman Levavi

1   3   5   7   9   10   8   6   4   2

First Edition

For Gail
Words can neither capture nor measure
my love and appreciation

Contents

Acknowledgments

Thank you to Edwene Gaines, whose book *The Four Spiritual Laws of Prosperity* first inspired me and others to leave behind the toxic habit of complaining. Thank you to Sam Mathes for the indelible imprint you have had on my life and this book. Thank you to Adam Khan, a gifted writer, for your observations, suggestions, and friendship. Thank you to Autumn Paige for conducting research that contributed greatly to this work. Thank you to Lia Bowen for sharing your insights and editing skills. Thank you to John Gladman for being a vast resource of talent and enthusiasm. Thank you to René Paré for being a friend, guide, and mentor. Thank you to Alice Anderson, John McLean, and Arlene Meyers for our top-tier relationship. Thank you to Joe Jacobson; none of this would be possible without the fellowship we share. Thank you to Dr. Robin Kowalski for your research and advice. Thank you to Vivien Jennings and Roger Doeren for your encouragement and support. Thank you to Bonnie Smith for your ideas and enthusiasm. Thank you to Teresa Loar for connecting *A Complaint Free*

World with people who have assisted us in spreading our mission. Thank you to Congressman Emanuel Cleaver, who understands the importance of focusing on what is constructive and unifying rather than what is destructive and divisive. Thank you to Steve Hanselman of Level 5 Media for gently, artfully, and professionally steering me through the publishing world. Thank you to Trace Murphy and the staff of Doubleday for your confidence and for sharing your wealth of talent and resources. Thank you to Jill Wendt, Herb Pierson, the hundreds of reporters and bloggers, and the many, many other people who have discovered the transformative impact of Complaint Free living and have given their time and energy to share this idea with others.

Thank you especially to Tom Alyea, who for more than three years has been the backbone of the Complaint Free Movement. You are a gift to me and to our world.

COMPLAINT FREE
RELATIONSHIPS

Introduction

Hell is other people.

—Jean-Paul Sartre

O ther people are our greatest gift.

Other people can be our greatest challenge.

Do a mental inventory. Better yet, pull out a piece of paper and write down every problem or challenge you are facing, every issue that concerns you—anything about which you have negative feelings or concerns. Then ask yourself, "How many of these problems involve other people?" Chances are the vast majority of struggles you face has to do with other people and could be improved by better relationships with them. Whether it is connecting at a deeper level with your intimate partner, convincing someone at work that your course of action is best, getting your children to do their chores, or explaining your needs to a salesclerk, most of our problems involve other people and could be resolved with successful, productive relationships. Even in support of large-scale global issues or causes, when you are able to build solid connections with others you are better able to influence positive change.

Our relationships with others can enhance every aspect of our lives or create untold stress. Our relationships can bring us pleasure as well as pain, comfort as well as conflict, peace as well as power struggles.

You may feel you are a victim in your relationships and powerless to improve them. You may even feel you are trapped in a spiral of negative, unhappy, and unfulfilling associations with others. But such is not the case. You are not a victim and you are not trapped. Beginning now, you can create the relationships you desire. You can transform your relationships with your significant other, friends, family, coworkers, and even casual acquaintances and begin to experience greater joy in these connections.

As you learn new relationship skills, you will begin to attract people to you who are warm, giving, helpful, agreeable, supportive, positive, and complimentary. And you will begin to draw out these same qualities in your existing relationships. Instead of complaining about how others are treating you, you will begin to create positive experiences that compound themselves and your life will vastly improve.

The genesis of what you will learn in this book began in July of 2006 when I presented an idea to my congregation. I am the lead minister at One Community Spiritual Center in Kansas City, Missouri. While teaching a series on manifesting prosperity, I handed out purple bracelets to be used as a tool to help eradicate complaining.

Our thoughts create our lives and our words indicate what we are thinking. Most people believe they are positive and optimistic. They think they are holding affirmative visions of ideal outcomes. In actuality, most people's thoughts are negative. Try as they may to think positively, most people's thoughts are decidedly bleak, as evidenced by their constant complaining. This propensity to think negatively plays out as dissatisfying life events and relationship.

The prolific mystery writer Agatha Christie once wrote, "Curious things, habits. People themselves never knew they had them." Truer words were never spoken, especially in regard to people's habitual complaining. Based on the information shared by people who have taken the Complaint Free challenge, the average person complains fifteen to thirty times a day and has no awareness he or she is doing so. Our Complaint Free bracelets have helped millions set a trap for their negativity by catching themselves in the act. Unlike the other ubiquitous silicone bracelets you see in every color of the rainbow, the ones we distribute are not to inform the world that the wearer supports a cause. Our purple bracelets are a tool to help people become aware of how often they complain and to begin to eradicate this negative and destructive form of communication from their lives.

The idea is simple: put the purple bracelet on either wrist and when (not if) you catch yourself complaining aloud, move the bracelet to the other wrist. With each complaint, the bracelet is to be moved from the current wrist to the other. In this process, you became aware of your negativity and, over a period of months, begin to complain less.

The goal is to complete 21 consecutive days without complaining. Scientists believe it takes 21 days for a new behavior to become habitual, so when you have gone 21 consecutive days without complaining, you will have reformatted your mental hard drive and being Complaint Free will be a new and enduring habit.

I first gave out 250 bracelets to my congregation but in short order the idea exploded around the world and what was a simple sermon tool has since become a worldwide movement. We have sent millions of purple bracelets to people in more than 105 countries and continue to send out tens of thousands each month. Thousands of individuals, families, churches, schools, prisons, therapists, hospitals, drug rehab centers, and businesses have embraced this program, with some amazing results.

A Complaint Free World split off from our church and is a

thriving nonreligious not-for-profit organization offering resources and tools to help people and organizations move beyond complaining to create a brighter reality.

We have been featured on *Oprah* and on every major television network in the United States as well as on many, many network and cable television shows around the world. Hundreds of newspapers both in the United States and internationally have done stories on us. Stories about us have appeared in dozens of magazines in the United States including *People* and *Newsweek*. Magazine publishers in the Netherlands and South Africa have included our purple bracelets in their magazines and have not only helped spread this concept and distribute bracelets but also seen their magazines' sales increase.

www.AComplaintFreeWorld.org

Companies have approached us wanting to distribute our bracelets with their products and have become official sponsors in their product arenas for what has become known as the Complaint Free Movement. My previous book, *A Complaint Free World: How to Stop Complaining and Start Enjoying the Life You Always Wanted,* which I wrote to answer the thousands of questions I was receiving by letter and email, became an international bestseller and continues to be published and read in more than a dozen countries around the world.

Not a day goes by that I don't receive several Google alerts of people blogging about their experiences with the Complaint Free challenge. I have been invited to deliver keynote addresses at dozens of conventions and conferences for many types of organizations, from federal agencies and Fortune 20 companies to schools, churches, hospitals, and civic organizations. This truly has become a phenomenon that continues to grow and expand and I am touched, honored, and amazed to be a part of it.

This is all very exciting. However, what is most gratifying are the thousands of people who have stayed with the challenge (and challenge it can be) to go 21 consecutive days without complaining. We have a link at our website, AComplaintFreeWorld.org, where people can let us know that they have completed 21 days without complaining, and we have received confirmation from people around the world who have made being Complaint Free a habit.

But one day, as I was sitting on a plane waiting to fly out to deliver a speech to several hundred corporate leaders about developing Complaint Free organizations, I had an epiphany. I was thinking about the Complaint Free program and was struck with what some might call a blinding flash of the obvious.

Yes, our lives are a reflection of our thoughts—this has been said by philosophers and leaders of every stripe for thousands of years. Yes, it's important for us to monitor what we are saying, as it indicates what we are thinking. Yes, this can be accomplished by the simple exercise of switching a bracelet from wrist to wrist until we become Complaint Free. All this is true.

> Extensive research shows that unhappy couples are distinguished from happy ones by the extent to which they reported their partner being argumentative, critical, and nagging— in other words, complaining.

The epiphany I experienced that day was that nearly all complaining is based on relationships.

Complaining is almost always about another person—a person with whom we are in some sort of relationship. The relationship may be formal, such as a marriage or work relationship, or it may be an informal relationship, such as with a customer we are serving or a person living in the next apartment. The relationship may be fleeting, such as with someone we pass in traffic, or it may span decades, such as our relationship with our family.

Because I am a minister, people often come to me for counseling and in nearly every case the challenge they are facing is a relationship challenge. In most of these counseling sessions, I discover that the relationship problems are either created or exacerbated by them complaining to or about the person with whom they share the relationship. As I delved into the subject, I discovered copious research has been done on the negative effects of complaining on relationships.

As early as 1938, a study by Lewis Terman showed that unhappy couples were distinguished from happy ones by the extent to which they reported their partner being argumentative, critical, and nagging (i.e., complaining). And in "A Descriptive Taxonomy of Couples' Complaint Interactions," originally published in the *Southern Speech Communication Journal* in 1989, Dr. J. K. Alberts states, "Diverse research indicates that negativity and negative communication are positively correlated with relational dissatisfaction." In other words, *unhappy relationships are most often distinguished by complaining.*

You may think, "But relationships are challenging, so why not complain?" Complaining gets out our frustrations so we don't have pent-up anger and resentment, right? Actually, the opposite is true and we'll discuss the "getting it out" myth in detail in this book.

Perhaps, rather than struggle, we could just give up on relationships—become the epitome of solitude and self-reliance. Then at least we wouldn't have to endure Sartre's "hell" of other people.

Sorry, that's not an option. We need relationships with others. Relationships are not simply something we want—relationships are a need.

Enrique Gutierrez immigrated to the United States from Cuba. While in Cuba, Enrique refused to sign on to the Castro regime's quashing of civil rights and exploiting the citizens of his beloved homeland. Enrique spoke out in favor of liberty and human rights. As a result, he was imprisoned in solitary confinement for more than a year. As he lay on the floor of his four-foot-by-six-foot cell, naked and with nothing but a rancid, threadbare blanket to stave off the cold, Enrique was in pain. The arresting officers had repeatedly and severely beaten him and, in the process, knocked out all of his teeth. His body was bruised and his bones were broken. Due to the poor nutrition offered at the prison, Enrique, who was already quite thin, had lost a great deal of weight and his skin had begun to crack and split at his elbows, shoulders, and knees, leaving festering, oozing sores.

His body was in relentless pain, yet Enrique told me that his greatest pain at that time was in his separation from other people. Not only did he miss his family but he was allowed no contact with any other human being and his soul cried out for connection.

We not only want to be in relationships with others, we crave our connections with them. Children who do not experience adequate human contact in their formative years can develop what is known as failure to thrive (FTT), in which their bodies fail to develop in normal, healthy ways. According to the University of Maryland Medical Center, one of the major contributing factors in FTT is often emotional deprivation. These children may experience the lack of an emotional relationship with others and their bodies respond to this deprivation by not growing properly.

The physical impact of a deficiency of relationships can be experienced at any age. Research has found that older people tend to visit doctors more often than younger people. Surely the decrepitude of age plays a part in this but studies have also found that a major reason older adults seek out doctors, chiropractors, and other health professionals is simply so that they can spend time with someone who gives them caring attention. Many of these older people have outlived their contemporaries, leaving their lives a wasteland void of human connection. Doctors and other professionals provide the relationship stimulation they hunger for.

Studies of other species support the idea that relationships are a need. Human beings often study chimpanzees, our closest evolutionary relatives, in an attempt to understand our own nature. In the simian world, the necessity of relationships is evident. A study on the enrichment of nonhuman primates by the National Institutes of Health found that chimps have a need for social interaction and relationships. Scientists there concluded, "While wild chimpanzees often spend part of the day alone, they are naturally social animals for whom constant solitude is a hardship."

Beyond needing connections and the pure joy of being with and sharing our life experiences with others, we also gain a great deal from our relationships.

A recent study conducted at Walter Reed Army Hospital found that approximately 17 percent of soldiers who were in battle but were not wounded suffer post-traumatic stress disorder (PTSD). Surprisingly, only 4 percent of soldiers—one out of every 25— who have been in battle and *were* seriously wounded (loss of an arm, leg, serious burns, paralysis, etc.) experience PTSD.

Doctors reviewing these statistics were surprised because they reasoned that a soldier who was badly wounded would have far greater challenges with post-traumatic stress. Why would a severely wounded soldier be 75 percent *less* likely to have lingering emotional challenges than one who was not wounded at all?

The researchers found that the answer to this perplexing question lay in therapy. Not psychological therapy but physical therapy; specifically, how physical therapy at Walter Reed was administered. Physical therapy at Walter Reed Army Hospital is conducted in one large room in which all of the wounded soldiers strive to return to a life resembling normalcy. As injured soldiers go through their daily physical therapy regimen, they see other soldiers, perhaps worse off than themselves, struggling to overcome their afflictions. Witnessing the other soldiers' efforts to recover, the soldiers become cheerleaders for one another. They encourage one another; they celebrate each other's smallest gains; they empathize deeply and let the other wounded soldiers know that they are pulling for them. The relationships created during their physical restoration help to heal their tortured psyches.

Relationships are the channels through which we receive the material things we desire as well. Every human being has hopes and dreams to which he or she aspires. Take a moment and reflect on the things you want. Ask yourself, "If I could have any of a thousand wishes, what would I like to have?"

Now, consider that everything you desire is either in the form of or possessed by another person. You may want a caring and supportive person with whom to share your life; that means a relationship. You may want a new car, fine home, or other luxury; you will need to earn the money for these things by serving other people and that means relationships. Relationships with others bring us everything we seek. It is imperative that we learn to get along with other people to achieve what we desire.

In *The Millionaire Mind,* author Thomas Stanley reports that of the thousands of self-made millionaires he interviewed, when they were asked, "What is the most important skill for attracting wealth?" fully 94 percent listed an ability to get along well with others as very or extremely important to wealth accumulation. In fact, *they rated the skill of creating healthy relationships with others as nearly five times more important to wealth creation than having above-average intelligence.* Your ability to get along with others will yield relationships that themselves can be more valuable than money. And your ability to cultivate and maintain relationships can bring you the material possessions you desire as well.

Complaining warps, weakens, and sometimes even destroys the very relationships that are vital to our happiness and well-being. When we engage in complaining, our relationships stagnate and devolve. Complaining shifts our focus from the positive attributes that drew us to the other person to what we perceive to be his or her faults. This shift draws us into a trap in which we feel unfulfilled and the other person feels inadequate.

My wife, Gail, used to work in an office where once a month several female employees would engage in what they called "group therapy." "Group therapy" meant going to a local Mexican restaurant, drinking several margaritas, and complaining vociferously about the men in their lives. The dominant theme seemed to be that "all men are dogs." Not surprisingly, none of these women was in a happy and sustaining relationship with a man.

Now, you might think that the women complained because their relationships with men were unfulfilling. But studies show that the opposite is true: their relationships with men were unfulfilling because they complained. Their focus was on the negative aspects of their relationships, and their commiseration about their challenges magnified their problems. Having spent the evening complaining about the "dogs" in their life, when these women arrived home they couldn't help but see Old Yeller sitting there in the La-Z-Boy. Their expectation, based on the case they had built in their heads, was that men were dogs. The women's husbands or boyfriends sensed this dissatisfaction and simply lived up (or, actually, down) to their expectations.

I once knew a very famous minister who confided, "Ministry would be great if only you didn't have to deal with people." Dealing with people can be a struggle filled with pain and sorrow but it needn't be so. The brilliant French philosopher and playwright Jean-Paul Sartre is known widely for the downbeat quote that begins this introduction—"Hell is other people." Late in life, Sartre explained, " 'Hell is other people' has always been misunderstood. It has been thought that what I meant by that was that our relations with other people are always poisoned, that they are invariably hellish relations. But what I really mean is something totally different. I mean that if relations with someone else are twisted, vitiated, then that other person can only be hell."

If your relations with others are twisted and vitiated (faulty), your relationships with them will seem like hell. You can straighten out twisted relationships. You can place them upon a solid foundation. You simply need to be open to new ideas and willing to allow these ideas to create new experiences. At the end of each chapter in this book you will find a section titled "Opening Up," which will give you exercises to more deeply integrate what you are learning. Some of these exercises include writing and you will gain much greater benefit from these exercises if you invest a moment to write down your answers on a piece of paper or in a journal.

If you're ready to move from hellish to harmonious connections, if you are ready to move from contemptuous to Complaint Free relationships, then let's get started.

CHAPTER 1

Relating in Relationships

Whatever I say must limit the world.

—Ludwig Wittgenstein

The word *relationship* stems from *relate*, which means "to recount or tell." Therefore, it could be said that a relationship is a human connection grounded in what we tell ourselves about another person; that is, what we relate to ourselves about that person. That inner dialogue defines and determines the course of our relationship.

> Relationship stems from *relate*, which means "to recount or tell."

When I was growing up, my dream was to become a radio announcer. In my freshman year of college I landed my first announcing job working for a station in my hometown of Columbia, South Carolina. I loved my job and over the course of several years I was promoted to production director for the station. As production director, my job was to mix music and sound effects into the commercials voiced by some of the greatest voice talents in our city.

Phil, an announcer some twenty years my senior with a deep,

resonant voice, had served as production director until senior management replaced him with me. Phil had an incredible voice—a "real set of pipes," in radio parlance. Phil wrote great ad copy, too, and he had a knack for selecting just the right music for a commercial. But Phil had come along during the early days of AM radio and ours was an FM station. Phil's skills had not kept pace with new technology, and although his commercials sounded fine on AM radio, in the rich, full sound of FM his productions sounded flat and tinny.

At first it was thrilling to mix commercials for Phil and the other talented announcers I had grown up listening to on the undisputed top radio station in our town. In time, however, I began to have problems working with Phil. Phil would tell me, and anyone who would listen, that the way I mixed commercials was careless and substandard. Phil did not like the way I catalogued the music. Phil did not like the way I filed copy. Phil did not like, it seemed, anything about me.

Over time, my appreciation for this icon of broadcasting crumbled into deep resentment. At first when Phil chastised me I would stare at the floor and mumble, "I'm sorry." In time, however, I began to defend myself and point out what I considered to be his inadequacies. Soon we were locked in frequent shouting matches hurling criticisms and insults at each other. Given that radio production booths have glass walls and are nearly soundproof, I can only imagine how ridiculous we looked to other employees as we stood, red-faced, mouthing all manner of insults that were seen by all but heard only by us.

One day, when we were locked in the middle of one of our heated arguments, Phil glanced at the studio clock and said, "I don't have time for your crap now—I'm having lunch with a friend." He stomped out of the production studio and down the hall, my eyes following him through the glass. There, waiting for him in the lobby, was a man about Phil's age. When he saw Phil, the man's face exploded into a grateful smile and he rushed to hug him.

As I watched Phil and this man exit the door of the radio station I was stunned. I can remember thinking, "Phil has friends? Phil's a jerk—how could Phil have friends?" That may sound strange, simplistic, and even arrogant, but it had never occurred to me that Phil could have friends. How could anyone actually *like* Phil?

I pondered this as I lay in bed that night. How could the other man derive such obvious pleasure from Phil's presence when I found him a constant source of irritation? Phil was a jerk, I told myself—end of story. "But if Phil is a jerk," I wondered, "why isn't he a jerk all the time with everyone?"

Phil's relationship with his friend was different from his relationship with me because Phil related (recounted or told) different things to himself about his friend than he did about me. Phil's internal dialogue was about the things he appreciated about his friend. Phil's pal also told himself positive things about Phil. I, on the other hand, experienced a constant, negative, judgmental voice shouting in my mind whenever I thought of Phil. "Phil is an obnoxious, opinionated, condescending jerk," I related to myself about him, and the result was that I had a relationship with a person who was all of those things. Phil's friend had a very different relationship with Phil because he related different things to himself about Phil.

How do I change other people?

The most common question I am asked is, "How do I change other people?" My experience with Phil gave me the answer to that question. Years later, I would meet Norm Heyder, a man I greatly admire who seems to know this secret instinctively. Norm has an uncanny ability to change other people. He has a capacity for standing his ground and presenting his opinions even in the midst of the most contentious interactions. Further, Norm is able to listen empathetically and dispassionately during a discussion. Norm and the other person may not always reach agreement or even meet on common ground but they always part as friends. If someone comes to Norm angry and irate, he or she leaves peaceful and content. In the face of staunch opinions and even vitriol, Norm has the ability to draw out the other person's rational and compassionate side, reflect it back, and then deal with that improved version of the same person. I once asked Norm how he is able to do this so consistently, and he said, "The only way to change someone is to change what you think about them."

A relationship is not just a surface interaction between two human beings. It is much more deep and complex. Other people sense the story we have created in our minds about them and they react accordingly. This is subconscious and instantaneous. It is something we all do all the time.

Think of someone you truly appreciate. What is it that you find appealing about this person? What do you relate to yourself about this person when you see or think of him or her? Do you characterize the person as genuine, giving, caring, helpful, courteous, upbeat, selfless, happy, or loving?

Next, call to mind a person who really bugs you—a person whose very name makes you grind your teeth. It could be anyone you really dislike: an ex-spouse, boss, neighbor, political leader, celebrity, or coworker. Ask yourself, "What am I telling myself about this person?" Be honest and free with your answers—let them flow without censoring or judging them. What is it about this person you really don't like? Do you see the person as rude, obnoxious, mean-spirited, selfish, opinionated, uncaring, unethical, conceited, stupid, oafish, or lazy?

Now consider this: the person you would place highest on the list of people you most cherish would probably be placed atop a "most-resented" list by someone else. And the person you find the most repellent would probably be placed at the peak of a "most-cherished" list by someone else.

I recently spoke at a very large seminar that spanned several days. During my presentation one woman interrupted my speech several times with questions and comments. I had only 60 minutes to present and was concerned I wouldn't get to cover everything I had prepared. Further, I found myself losing my place with each interruption. As I watched the other speakers over the next couple of days, I noticed she did the same thing to them. They were as visibly distracted and frustrated as I had been. I found that I related to myself that the woman was rude, thoughtless, and irritating.

After the seminar concluded, I went to the airport and purchased some dinner at a take-out restaurant to eat prior to my flight. I looked around for a place to sit but found no empty tables. A woman saw me standing there and invited me to share an empty seat at her table. Although I didn't recognize her, she told me that she had attended the seminar as a guest of her best friend. She talked at length about how generous, giving, thoughtful, and caring her friend was. She shared touching stories about her friend and the great philanthropic work her friend was doing.

Well, you guessed it—my dinner companion's friend was the very same woman I had found rude, thoughtless, and irritating. What she told me completely reshaped my experience of the woman. I began to tell myself different things about her and now find I have similarly warm feelings toward her. Further, I or one of the other speakers could have solved the problem by owning our experience with her and speaking to her privately, asking her to keep her questions and comments to the allotted Q&A sessions.

Think of someone you find truly loathsome. Now ask yourself: does this person have friends or family who love and appreciate—even cherish—him or her? If you're honest, in nearly every case the answer is yes. Ask yourself what this person's friends or family say to themselves about him or her. Picture in your mind this person's greatest, most appreciative supporter and ask what he or she values in this person.

Whew! This is tough. Our minds don't want to go there. Our minds want to write the person off. It makes us feel better to pigeonhole the other person in a way that makes him or her bad and us good.

> **You are constantly relating to yourself about everyone. Just this awareness will unravel complex and challenging relationships.**

To have Complaint Free relationships we must understand that relationships stem from what we relate to ourselves about other people. You needn't *begin* to relate to yourself about others; you are *already* doing it all the time. Just the awareness that you do this begins to unravel the complex and often challenging opinions you have created about those with whom you share relationships.

In *Hamlet,* Shakespeare wrote, "There is nothing either good or bad, but thinking makes it so." Imagine for a moment that everything you think about another person is exactly that and nothing more—something *you* think. It is something you have fabricated and accepted as fact in your head. This is true for the people you most appreciate and those you find most irritating. People are neither good nor bad but our thinking makes them so—for us.

I realized that Phil was Phil—neither good nor bad. He was a very different version of Phil with me than with his friend but the kind, giving, joyous Phil enjoyed by others was there whether it manifested itself in my presence or not. His friend drew out these qualities by the thoughts he held about Phil.

With this new awareness, I knocked tentatively at the open door to Phil's office. Phil glared up contemptuously from his typewriter. "Phil, you started out in radio as a young man about my age, right?" I said.

"Yeah," he growled. "I've been in this business longer than you've been alive."

My first thought was that he was taking a shot at me for being inexperienced. But then I thought, "The nice Phil would never say something unkind and I'm here to see the nice Phil." I took a deep breath and asked, "What was it like when you first started in this business?"

Phil stared at me for a long moment as if trying to figure out what I was up to. Without invitation I slid into the chair opposite his desk and did my best, for the first time in years, to smile at him. Slowly Phil began to smile back and share with me a tidbit or two about the "good old days" of radio.

What began as the melting of a glacier soon became a spring torrent as Phil told me many a fascinating tale. He told me that the first radio station he worked for didn't even have audio tape—they recorded on audio wire, which came in long spools. To make an edit in the wire they would touch the lit end of a cigarette to the wire and melt through it, remove any unwanted sections, and then press the warm, soft copper ends together. "I think this is one reason I've never been able to give up cigarettes," he said, waving his hand, which always seemed to hold a lit Winston. "Smokes and radio—they just go together, you know?"

Four and a half hours—that's how long I sat in Phil's office. He told me behind-the-scenes stories about the great announcers I'd idolized as a young boy. I didn't feign interest; I didn't have to. I was riveted in place. I wasn't trying to make Phil feel good. I was reveling in the stories he shared about a medium he and I both loved. Around ten o'clock that night Phil and I both looked at the clock and realized we had work to do to prepare for the next broadcast day. But in our conversation I'd not only healed a relationship with a coworker but reclaimed a childhood hero.

Things were different from that point forward. I realized that when Phil offered advice he wasn't challenging my competence, even if his tone was didactic. I developed compassion for him, knowing he was expressing a deep need to still be relevant in an industry that seemed to be passing him by. As a result, I found I no longer needed to justify myself or prove myself superior to him. Rather than trying to show him up with my expertise in what was then new technology, I asked his opinion and, most important, I listened. I changed what I related to myself about Phil and as a result our relationship changed.

> Having Complaint Free relationships is not about learning what to *do*; it is about learning how to *be*.

Do you want to change other people? You can. The question is whether you are willing to do what is necessary. Having healthy and happy relationships is not about learning a bunch of tricks so you can manipulate others. The results of such techniques are often short-lived.

Having Complaint Free relationships is not about learning what to *do;* it is about learning how to *be.* When you become the kind of person for whom such relationships are common, others shift in your presence.

To change someone else you must first change how you relate to yourself about that person. This is where it all begins. You must change what the voice inside your head is saying. You must take responsibility for and be willing to transform your inner dialogue, which is setting the tone of your relationship.

You may be hearing that very same voice now as you read. It may be telling you that this approach is simplistic or naive. Further, that voice may be demanding to know why you should have to change. *You're* not the problem, you think—*they* are! This voice was best summed up by a woman who emailed me about her relationship problems with her husband. When I emailed her back suggestions of things she might do to improve her situation with him, she responded angrily, "Why should I be the one to change and my husband be allowed to get away with his behavior?"

What this woman does not understand is that in many ways *her husband's behavior is a reaction to her behavior toward him*. And her behavior stems from what she is relating to herself about him. Just as Phil was very different with his friend than he was with me, the people in your life are different with other people. Why? Because others tell themselves different things about those people and they respond accordingly. Others relate observations about these people different from the ones you tell yourself; people sense this and react to fit the role ascribed to them.

What is the one thing common to all of your relationships? In every connection you have with any and every other human being you will ever encounter, what is the one unchanging constant? The answer is, of course, *you*. You are a primary ingredient in every relationship you will ever have. Take yourself out of the relationship and there is no relationship. If by altering what you tell yourself about the other person you change how you relate in the relationship, the dynamics of the relationship shift. You can spend your life waiting, complaining, and insisting that the other person change, with little or no result. Or you can realize that the experience you are having of the other person is one of many possible scenarios available to you, and you can begin to focus on and create the relationship partner you wish to experience.

The first thing you must do is understand that *you are already doing this*. You are relating to yourself information about every person you encounter. You do this continuously and unconsciously. Other people sense your bearing toward them and respond in kind.

Recently I was staying at a hotel in Austin, Texas. Unlike many hotels in which I've stayed, there were two exterior doors leading to my room. The first door opened from the main hotel hallway into a narrow foyer; inside the foyer, two doors opened into two different suites, mine and that of the people who were staying in the suite adjacent to mine.

Several times throughout the day I went in and out of my suite, each time allowing the doors of both my suite and the outer foyer to close unassisted by me. Around six in the evening I left my room to attend a reception with my hosts. Again I allowed the weight of both doors to close them. As I was walking toward the elevator I heard a woman shout from behind me, "You are the most inconsiderate man I have ever met." I looked around to see whom this woman was yelling at and was surprised to find that she was addressing me. She continued, "All day long you have been intentionally slamming these doors and you're driving me crazy! Slam! Slam! Slam! You are inconsiderate and rude!"

Then, with her words dripping with sarcasm, she grasped the handle of the outer door and in an overly dramatic fashion demonstrated how she felt I should close the doors. Slowly and deliberately she began opening and closing the door, saying, "See? It's very simple: open, close, open, close, open, close!"

I muttered an apology and smiled as she stomped back into her suite.

As I pressed the elevator button, I thought about my relationship with this woman. Just moments earlier we had not met and so in my mind there *was* no relationship. But in her mind, our relationship had been ongoing for quite some time and it had a very unpleasant tone. To her I was the "rude and inconsiderate" man next door. From her anger, it seemed she had been having quite a conversation in her head about me. She was relating to herself what type of person I must be and had built up a head of steam that burst forth in angry and condescending words when she finally saw me.

As I rode the elevator I found myself beginning to relate

thoughts to myself about her. In the short time it took for a non-stop elevator ride from the sixth to the eighteenth floor, I told my-self a great many things about this woman—angry, judgmental, and critical things. I began to look forward to returning to my room later that night. "She thought I was slamming the doors be-fore? I'll show her door slamming," I thought, my blood pressure and anger rising along with the elevator.

As I stepped out on the eighteenth floor, I stopped for a mo-ment and realized that I was not immune to creating a complain-ing relationship in my head. I had built a judgmental case in my mind about this woman and was now ready to react in accordance with my thoughts. The case was so strong and I felt so right that I was eager to *really* slam those doors. I felt justified reacting this way even though I knew I would be embarrassed later if I did slam the doors. I also knew this would do nothing to lessen my upset or improve our relationship.

This was not how I wanted to be. Regardless of how she acted toward me, I had a choice. I could improve this relationship even if I was the only one making an effort to do so. The first step toward turning this around was to realize that I was indeed telling myself a story about her and that I could choose to tell myself something different. This is always the first step. You need to be-come aware that you are relating a story to yourself about the other person.

I then began to consider reasons for her behavior. What if she had been up the previous night with a terminally ill son or daugh-ter at a local hospital? The stress of this would certainly make her hypersensitive to the sound of the doors closing. Or what if she had just found out her husband was cheating on her? Her anger could have been misdirected at me.

My neighbor at the hotel had created a story about me based on her experiences of me but I did not have to respond in kind—or rather, unkind. The first step to changing an internal story is realizing we are telling ourselves one and then we can choose to relate something different.

Because I was speaking the next day to a group of people on the importance of living a Complaint Free life, I soon began to think how comical it was that this woman had complained so stridently to the "no-complaint guy." In no time, I began to see the humor in this and found myself laughing out loud. Rather than an enemy, this woman became an ally of sorts. She had given me a great example to share when I spoke. Rather than create a story in my head that made me right and her wrong, I related a story to myself that invited me to empathize with her rather than want to take revenge on her for her treatment of me.

> Assumptions are the termites of relationships.
> —HENRY WINKLER

As I went into my room that night, I closed each door gently.

The following morning I was sitting outside enjoying a cup of coffee when the woman's husband approached, introduced himself, and thanked me not only for closing the doors more quietly but for not reacting angrily to his wife. "She's been under a lot of strain lately," he said. "It's just not like her to behave that way. I'm really sorry."

Although my reactive human mind initially had wanted to write her off as being a querulous, nagging, petty, condescending shrew, the truth was more in line with the empathic story I had created for myself. Even if I had not found out that she was indeed under a lot of strain, I still would have found peace in the midst of turmoil. And isn't that what we really want?

Your relationships all stem from what you are relating to yourself about the other people in your life. Relationships are an outer expression of the judgments you make about others and the stories you create based on them. This is not a new phenomenon; it has gone on since human beings first appeared. In fact, one of the oldest stories in our culture points out our natural propensity for making judgments.

The allegory of Adam and Eve in the Bible says that the couple lived together in paradise. Think about that for a moment—a couple living together in absolute bliss. But something happened that caused them to leave this idyllic state.

In the story, the pair was told they could enjoy all of Eden with the exception of one thing: they were not to eat from the Tree of the Knowledge of Good and Evil. It wasn't an apple tree that they were forbidden to partake of; it was the Tree of the Knowledge of Good and Evil. What does it mean to eat from the Tree of the Knowledge of Good and Evil? It means we gain knowledge (relate to ourselves) that one thing is good and another thing is evil. Eating from the fruit of the Tree of the Knowledge of Good and Evil means we relate to ourselves that one thing is good and another bad.

Adam and Eve committed the original sin and as a result found themselves evicted from paradise. And this is the original sin: *to judge.* Once we judge a person as being bad we begin to build a case for this judgment in our heads. We relate, over and over, the substantiating evidence for this belief and the other person is then seen in all our interactions as possessing these negative traits. Relationships based on negativity cannot exist in paradise.

There is an old story of two tribes of people who lived on either side of a yawning gorge. They wanted to build a bridge to connect their communities but the gorge was so wide and steep they could not think of a way to bridge it. In time an idea came to someone on one side. He tied a string to an arrow and attached a note to the arrow's shaft. He then shot the arrow to a safe spot on the other side of the chasm to be found by the villagers there.

Once the villagers on the other side recovered the arrow they read the note. It said, "Tie a string to the thread and we will pull it back across. Then we will tie a piece of yarn to the string for you to pull back to your side. Then you tie a rope to the yarn and we will pull it back." Through this action of pulling first a thread, then a piece of string, then a piece of yarn, then a light piece of rope, then heavier rope, then still heavier rope upon which they built a bridge, they were able to connect with each other.

Relationships are joined in much the same way. We pull to our-selves meaning based on what we see the other person doing. The other person then pulls back meaning to him- or herself based on what we do. Back and forth this energetic interplay moves, each time reinforcing our preconceptions. Like two submarines ping-ing sonar and then attempting to maneuver about based on the other's position, we relate and react, relate and react.

This process is automatic and continual and because we don't realize we are doing it, we feel we have little if any control. This explains how you can find yourself in the middle of an argument with someone and have no idea how you got there. The inner communication threads cause us to react in ways that rapidly mul-tiply on themselves.

We tend to think of relationships as the interactions between human beings but the interactions are the expression of the rela-tionship, not the relationship itself. The true relationship is the relating that is going on in the minds of the two people—the threads, strings, yarns, and ropes that get pulled back and forth.

Whether we are assigning positive or negative meaning to the interaction determines how we will respond and this response cre-ates meaning in the other person's mind. These intertwining threads of inner communication can become strands that bind us in happy relationships or they can become a noose around the neck of the relationship.

In 1946 Viktor Frankl published his classic book *Man's Search for Meaning,* which chronicles his experiences as a concentration camp inmate. Frankl found that those who survived the horrors of

Nazi internment had a similar characteristic: they had a reason to live. Their lives continued to have meaning. Regardless of their loss of family, physical torture, and interminable imprisonment, if prisoners had a reason to live—if they had meaning for their lives—then they were far more likely to survive this devastating experience.

We all search for meaning, for relevance. The human mind thrives on things making sense. Whether we are looking for a meaning to our lives that transcends being in a Nazi concentration camp or we are looking for an understanding as to why someone treated us in the manner they did, our minds are meaning-making machines.

The word *mean* has several definitions. Primarily it means "significance" or "intention," as in "What does this mean?" or "What do you mean by that?" Another of the definitions for *mean* is "unkind." Far too often when we are relating the meaning of another's actions to ourselves we extend the word to its definition of "unkind." We assume that what they "mean" is to be "mean" or unkind.

Our meaning-making machines decide that the other person is, well, mean!

In the 1970s, a new field of psychology emerged called "narrative psychology." Narrative psychology holds that our identities are shaped by the accounts of our lives found in the stories (narratives) we create. Dan McAdams, a pioneer in the field of narrative psychology, said, "We are all tellers of tales, and we seek to provide our scattered and often confusing experiences with a sense of coherence by arranging the episodes of our lives." In other words, we relate to ourselves a meaningful story about the events of our lives. Random events that have little or no connection to each other

> When we observe another's actions and assign "meaning," we often assume that what they "mean" is to be "mean" or unkind.

are dots that we connect into a story—a story that provides rational, if not accurate, meaning for us.

We accept as true the story we have created and then we look for experiences that reinforce the narrative. If we feel a person we know has treated us unkindly in the past, or if someone in a similar position such as a spouse, boss, or clerk has treated us unkindly, or even if someone who resembles the person with whom we are interacting has treated us unkindly, we assume the worst. Our defenses go up. We prepare for battle and the other person, sensing this, responds in that way when dealing with us. It happens so quickly on both sides that neither is aware of what has caused the situation and both react and compound the experience, reinforcing it as they go along.

Have you ever been around a person who you can tell does not like you? We've all been in a situation where people have made up their minds about us based on a story they have related to themselves about us. They have concluded that we are a certain way and we sense this in their presence. Everything we do seems to reinforce the judgments they have made about us. It feels uncomfortable. It feels unfair. We feel misjudged, maligned, attacked.

So what do people do when they feel attacked? They counterattack. They gather their army of thoughts and their munitions of assumptions and meet in the battlefield of their own minds. They begin to ascribe all manner of negative attributes to the other person. Rather than allowing the other person's opinions to be just that—opinions—they feel compelled to create stories in their heads vilifying the other person. "She doesn't like me? Well, that's because she's just a clerk at a store. She's too stupid to get a real job!" And the threads begin to weave.

For every person in your life, you are playing Santa Claus. You are deciding whether he or she belongs on the "naughty" list or the "nice" list. And yet your distinctions are true only for you; others do not necessarily share your opinion of this person. Your judgments about the person are stories you have created and have no more foundation in reality than Santa Claus himself.

I'm not saying you should not seek to discern what is best for yourself. For the survival of our species, it is important for us to discern what is healthy and helpful and distinguish it from what is destructive and dangerous. It is a sad fact that some people, because of their own challenges, act out in ways that make them unhealthy or unsafe to be around. They may be violent, critical, unethical, or otherwise dangerous. These are people for whom we should have compassion, knowing that something must have happened in their lives that hurt them deeply and causes them to act out as they do. People who hurt others are hurting people. Hurt people hurt people. We are not being judgmental by separating ourselves from such people. But we should do so with compassion.

> We accept as true the story we have created and then we look for experiences that reinforce our narrative.

Compassion is defined as "a keen awareness of the suffering of another coupled with a desire to see it relieved." People hurt others as a result of their own inner strife and pain. Avoid the reactive response of believing they are bad; they already think so and are acting that way. They aren't bad; they are damaged and they deserve compassion.

Note that compassion is an internal process, an understanding of the painful and troubled road trod by another. It is not trying to change or fix that person. It may mean reaching out a hand to that person but it does not mean repeatedly putting your hand out to be bitten. That is not compassion. Every person is on his or her own journey and is not here for us to fix. Thinking you need to fix someone is a judgment. Desire to see the suffering of another relieved, but realize that it is not up to you to change that person. Constantly trying to actively intervene in another's suffering is not compassion.

Discern if someone's presence in your life helps your soul grow, helps you experience more joy and more of the goodness in the world, helps you to discover your own innate beauty and wonder. If not, bless that person and release him or her with no need for judgment.

Discernment is not judgment. Discernment is determining what will not only protect you but fulfill you and bring you happiness. Judgment, on the other hand, comes from a need to build a case to prove to your inner voice that the decision you have made is the correct one. Judgment is used to seek validation for your decision. Judgment and anger result from a need to prove you are right when at your core you know you probably are not. French novelist and playwright Victor Hugo wrote, "Strong and bitter words indicate a weak cause." You seek to make your weak cause strong through harsh condemnation of the other person. All of this happens in the true realm of all relationships: your mind.

> Strong and bitter words indicate a weak cause.
>
> —VICTOR HUGO

The concept of New Year's Eve is fascinating. Based on a construct that human beings created and that we have all agreed upon—the calendar—we cross over from one year to another at the stroke of midnight on the mutually agreed upon day, December 31. The arrival of the New Year is met with resounding celebration and much anticipation for improvements in our lives. "Happy New Year!" we shout to anybody and everybody. We resolve that our lives are going to vastly improve over the next 365 days and we expect great things. The coming year is going to be terrific and we can't wait for it to arrive. We have a symbol in the United States of a bright, happy baby to represent the burgeoning New Year, whereas we see the waning year as a withered, tired old man. Not only is the old year something we are ready to release but we can't wait for it to be over and done with.

The irony, of course, is that the year that is concluding is the very same year we jubilantly welcomed in just 12 months earlier. When that year came into being, based on our agreement that it came into being—remember, the calendar is nothing more than a system created by and agreed upon by people—we were not only filled with joy but certain that it would bring all manner of great things. And now we celebrate its passing as if it were rotting fish being carted off to a garbage dump.

What makes the difference between December 31 and, say, May 10? What's the difference between one year and another? The difference is the stories we tell ourselves—the meaning we ascribe, what we relate to ourselves. We tell ourselves that the coming year presents a beacon of hope for health and abundance and we celebrate that potential. Then, just a few months into that New Year, our old stories about our lives begin to kick in. We begin to live out the narrative we have created about our existence and the momentum of our lives kicks in like a tidal wave crushing and drowning our aspirations for the New Year. That is, until the next New Year arrives and we repeat the process.

> What you say, goes—but only for you and those who agree with you.
> —THADDEUS GOLAS

We are living, breathing examples of narrative psychology. Psychologist Dan McAdams notes, "Starting in late adolescence, we manufacture our dramatic personal myths by selectively mining some experiences and neglecting or forgetting others." And Thaddeus Golas put it this way in *The Lazy Man's Guide to Enlightenment:* "What you say, goes—but only for you and those who agree with you."

If you are truly ready to transform your relationships, you must embrace that you are a major causal factor in your relationships. Your relationships with others are a projection of the stories you tell yourself about the people in your life. You can change the stories you relate to yourself about another. By changing your narrative about another person, by putting him or her at the top of your "nice" rather than "naughty" list, your relationship with that person will change.

Several years ago, my wife, Gail, and I were driving home from a dinner with friends. We were traveling in separate cars with me in the lead. Although Gail was not far behind me, as I looked back in my mirror I noticed that I had trouble seeing her following me. The lights on her car seemed to be very dim. I was concerned for her safety because I thought other cars might not be able to see her coming.

When we arrived at home, I told Gail about her dim headlights. She admitted having trouble seeing the road ahead of her at night and that her headlights had been getting progressively weaker for nearly a year.

"I thought headlight bulbs went out all at once," she said. "I didn't think they dimmed out slowly over time." I agreed that I had never heard of headlights dimming slowly and we wondered if the problem might be more serious than just bulbs; perhaps the car's electrical system was going bad.

We dropped the car off at our local mechanic's the next day. When I asked the mechanic how much we owed him for the repair, he said, "Nothing."

"Nothing?" I asked. "Why not?"

"There was nothing wrong with the bulbs or the electrical system," he explained. "Your headlights were just dirty." Gail is one of those people who pride themselves on keeping their car clean, so I didn't see how this was possible. The mechanic read the confusion on my face and said, "Your wife's car has pop-up headlights. When she drives at night the headlights are on and, therefore, up—bugs, road grime, and other stuff stick to them."

"But she washes her car every week," I said.

"Well, unless she washes the car with the headlights on so they pop up, the lenses aren't getting clean. The junk builds up over time and makes the headlights grow dim."

Think about the relationships that are challenging to you. On the outside you might think that you have tried everything you can to improve them. Perhaps you consciously smile when you are with the other person. Perhaps you've done things that you thought might please the other person. Yet nothing has worked. You have washed the outside of the car but the headlights are still not showing a bright light coming from you. The real issue is not on the outside; it's what is going on inside. Over time you have related to yourself a narrative and this is how this person is for you. But he or she is not necessarily this way with others. You can change your stories and, in so doing, transform your relationships.

"What am I telling myself about this person?"

About now you may be asking, "Are you suggesting I constantly ask myself what I'm saying to myself about everyone I encounter?"

Yes, I am.

Whenever you are with someone, break through the default haze of reactive story creation by asking yourself what you are relating internally about that person. Just doing this will make you aware that you are indeed creating narratives about everyone and this will afford you the chance to form thoughts about others intentionally rather than reactively. Again, you are already relating things to yourself about every person in your life. Become aware of this by asking yourself, "What am I telling myself about this person?"

"But won't constantly asking myself what I'm thinking about everyone I meet drive me crazy?" No, you're *already* crazy. What better definition of *crazy* is there than letting your mind run amok unchecked? This is your first step toward sanity and, more important, toward happy relationships.

Venerable spiritual guide and author Thich Nhat Hanh wrote,

When you plant lettuce, if it does not grow well, you don't blame the lettuce. You look for reasons it is not doing well. It may need fertilizer, or more water, or less sun. You never blame the lettuce. Yet if we have problems with our friends or our family, we blame the other person. But if we know how to take care of them, they will grow well, like the lettuce. Blaming has no positive effect at all, nor does trying to persuade using reason and argument. That is my experience. If you understand, and you show that you understand, you can love, and the situation will change.

Opening Up

1. Think of someone with whom you have a happy and satisfying relationship. Write down what you tell yourself about this person.
2. Think of someone with whom you struggle. Write down what you relate to yourself about this person.
3. Considering the person you find challenging, what would people who have a satisfying relationship with this person tell themselves about him or her? Write down things this person's best friend, mother, or other admirer might say about him or her.
4. The next time you are with this person you experience as challenging, actively hold thoughts of appreciation and admiration, attempting to see him or her as someone who belongs atop your "nice" list.
5. Whenever you are with someone, ask yourself, "What am I relating to myself about this person?"

CHAPTER 2

When Worlds Collide

*When you argue with reality, you lose—but only
100 percent of the time.*

—Byron Katie

The other day I awoke to find myself in a great mood. I bounced into the kitchen to make some coffee. While there, I stood for several minutes to drink in the morning air wafting through the open windows. I watched with joy as the horses grazed and the birds feasted at the bird feeder. I felt bright and cheery. I then went outside to feed our dogs. While there, I petted and talked with them at length.

I went back in the house, poured my coffee, and began my morning ritual. I had a full day ahead but time seemed to move along comfortably as I meditated, exercised, cooked and ate breakfast, returned some emails, made phone calls, showered, dressed, and drove to the office. All was well. I felt bright and happy, positively buoyant.

The rest of the day followed suit. I handled everything that came my way with ease and joy. I had numerous satisfying interactions with my friends and colleagues and returned home to have a wonderful evening with my wife and daughter. It was a splendid day.

The next morning, it was like someone had pulled the plug on whatever magic had surrounded my life just 24 hours earlier. I awoke feeling anxious and gloomy. Feeding our pets was a chore rather than a joy. Throughout the day I seemed to be running late for everything. It felt like I couldn't communicate clearly with those I spoke with and small inconveniences felt overly irritating. I was truly glad when the day was over.

Nothing particularly bad happened between that first day and the next to cause the shift. I was simply in a very different space emotionally on each of the two days and I'm not sure what caused me to go from Dr. Jekyll one day to "If you see me, you'd better hide" the next. I hadn't changed my routine. I ate and exercised as I had the day before. I took my nutritional supplements as I always do. I meditated. But something was off the second day when compared to how I'd felt the day before.

This is a universal occurrence. You have experienced this yourself whether or not you took notice. Who we are changes. You are different from one day to the next. This change of state can be influenced by myriad things. The amount and quality of sleep you receive can impact how you show up in the world. So can the quantity and type of food you eat as well as how much you exercise. The interactions you have with others can change your mood and condition, too. The weather can cause you to feel and act different. Even the content of your dreams can affect who you are in a given moment.

One morning I awoke to find my typically upbeat wife in a sour mood. When I asked Gail what was troubling her she looked at me angrily and said, "You cheated on me." Shock raced across my face, but even before I could deny her accusation, she added, "Last night, in a dream I had, you cheated on me. I'm sorry; I know it was just a dream. I should just shake it off but I'm having trouble letting it go."

The Taoists have a saying, "You can never step into the same stream twice." The stream is always flowing. When you stand at the edge of a stream, the water that is before you is not the same water that was there even seconds earlier nor is it the water that will be beneath your feet seconds from now. The water is always moving. What you call the stream is still there. But the content of the stream is always changing, always in flux. The same is true for people. Each day—indeed, each moment—we are subtly (and sometimes not so subtly) different.

> You can't step into the same stream twice.
> —TAOIST SAYING

The impact of this can be seen in our relationships. If people are constantly changing, then relationships are built on a foundation of tectonic plates that are always shifting, always realigning. This can be a beautiful and incredible dance of discovery or it can be an earthquake causing incredible destruction.

There is an old maxim I regularly share with couples when they come to me for premarital counseling:

> *A man marries a woman thinking she will never change.*
> *A woman marries a man thinking she can change him.*
> *They are both wrong.*

Everyone is always changing. Everyone is different in any given moment than in any other given moment. People may or may not change to our liking, and if we think we can direct the course of this change without resistance, we are mistaken.

Change is ongoing and inevitable—for ourselves as well as others. We are never standing still. If we celebrate the change, our relationships deepen. If we focus on change as something to be marveled at rather than seeing it as a threat to the relationship, it creates new areas of exploration within the relationship. Rather than needing to go outside the relationship to find new experiences, new connections, new meaning, and new growth, we can find it within our existing connection.

Oftentimes people explain the end of a relationship by saying, "We have grown apart." Although most of our body parts cease to grow once we reach the adult-sized version of our physical selves, our spirit grows as long as we are alive. As it does, it reshapes who we are. We are different people. When people "grow apart" it's likely they have begun to focus on their differences rather than on what attracted them to the other person in the first place. And if some of those attributes that originally drew them to each other have transformed, they may not be open to appreciating the new and wonderful things about the other person. When asked about his relationship with his wife, photorealist artist Chuck Close said, "I've been married for forty years. It's not one marriage—by then you've had four or five totally different marriages. And you hope that you evolve in similar ways, in compatible ways, and that you now have new reasons to be with them. But it's going to be different from the previous reasons to be with them."

When a man selects a tie he first looks at the suit he wishes to wear. What subtle colors and shades are woven into the suit that he would like the tie to draw out? He then looks for a tie that is compatible with those aspects of the suit—a tie that draws out those colors. Does every color in the tie have to match every color in the suit? Of course not; in fact, that makes the combination look contrived and unappealing. It becomes forced, stagy. The colors and patterns of the tie should complement the suit, not be redundant with it.

Imagine a tie/suit combination that a man selects and wears to work. In the early afternoon he glances in the mirror and this time, rather than his focus being on the colors in the tie that complement the suit, his focus shifts to the colors that clash. Even though there may be far more colors that complement the suit than do not, if his attention is on how the pairing doesn't go together more than how it does, he will not be as content with the relationship between the two.

Our relationships with others change because we change and they change. When this happens, we can focus on what no longer matches or we can instead look more deeply at what seemed to make us compatible in the first place. We can look at the colors in the suit/tie combination that still go together. Moreover, we can look for new compatibilities that we had not seen earlier because they had not existed.

The day I mentioned at the beginning of this chapter that seemed to be so trying, taxing, and difficult was made all the more so coming on the heels of the previous day, which had felt so light, breezy, and joyful. *It was the comparison between the two days that made the second day seem so unbearable.* On that second, less upbeat day, I kept asking myself questions such as:

"What's wrong with me today?"
"Why don't I feel as good today as I did yesterday?"
"How do I get myself back to where I was yesterday?"

Over and over I asked questions that invoked negative comparisons between the second day and the first. The second day was, in my mind, "bad," "wrong," "a downer," and so on. My questions emphasized this disparity and reinforced this position.

I once attended a seminar where the speaker asked, "What is the best way to hold another person's attention?" All in attendance sat quietly waiting for the answer. He repeated, "What is the best way to hold another person's attention?" Our interest was full on the presenter and the anticipation grew as we awaited the secret. Again he said, "What is the best way to hold another person's attention?" Now, sensing he wanted a response, audience members began to shout out possible answers to the question. Ignoring their comments, he repeated yet again, "What is the best way to hold another person's attention?" This went on for several minutes until we realized that he had been demonstrating the answer the entire time. Not a single one of us had experienced our minds wandering during this exercise. The answer was what the speaker was repeatedly doing—asking questions. When we ask questions we engage the mind; we focus.

In your relationships, what is your focus? Are you asking yourself questions that draw you to the other person or that repel you from him or her? Are you asking what you like about the person or what you dislike? Are you asking what you appreciate about the person or what you would like to change? Are you asking how you can make the person happy or why he or she is not making you happy?

In chapter 1 we discussed how relationships are an expression of what we relate to ourselves about another person. What directs this relating or telling? The questions you are asking yourself about the other person.

Are you asking yourself why some of the colors in the tie don't match the suit or are you asking yourself which colors complement the suit and, in so doing, enjoying the pairing of the two?

I have to admit that for the first several years of our relationship I had a list of things about my wife, Gail, that I wished were different and I frequently asked myself questions that reinforced them. "I like to ride roller coasters, play racquetball, and scuba-dive—why isn't she more adventurous? I am a very gregarious person and like to talk things out—why isn't she more talkative?"

I was confusing our differences with incompatibilities. The word *compatible* is defined as "able to exist and perform in harmonious or agreeable combination." You do not need to have a lot in common to exist in a harmonious combination. In fact, when we stop focusing on our differences as something lacking in the relationship, our diversity can create harmony. Beautiful and melodious vocal harmony is created when singers each sing at a *different* pitch, not the same one. It is the differences, not the similarities, in the range of their voices that creates the harmony.

"How are we able to exist and perform in a harmonious and agreeable way?"

Don't confuse differences with compatibilities. If you are having a challenge with someone, engage your mind with the compatibility question. Ask yourself repeatedly, "How are we able to exist and perform in a harmonious and agreeable way?" As you ask this question, the answers will come.

People often think that if their distinct personalities and desires are not reflected back in a person with whom they are in a relationship, there must be something wrong. This is because most people are insecure about themselves and need reinforcement of their own value and worth. If they don't see their interests and tastes mirrored by others, they worry that there must be something wrong.

A couple once came to me for counseling. During our conversation I discovered how diverse their personalities and interests were. He is extroverted. He enjoys hiking, skiing, and model trains. She, on the other hand, is a consummate introvert. She loves reading, crossword puzzles, listening to music, and yoga. They enjoy a lot of quality time as a family with their three small children but they don't share a lot of hobbies.

The wife conceded that they enjoyed special times together but complained that her husband did not join her in her favorite activities. The husband responded, "I am happy to do the things she wants to do but she gets upset." The husband said that he had told his wife on numerous occasions, "I'll do whatever you want to do. Just name it; I'll do whatever you like."

She looked into his eyes, then into mine, and finally down at her shoes as she admitted, "I don't want you just to do things I like to do—I want you to *want* to do the things I like to do." She saw their differences as incompatibilities. I suggested that if he spent time with her in a new activity, he might come to enjoy it. If not, he would be sharing with her the greatest gifts one can give: time and attention.

All of us have our idiosyncrasies, those things that make us unique. It is harmful to relationships when we begin to look at a person's idiosyncrasies and call them faults. What we need is an appreciation for our similarities as well as our differences and an understanding that these differences do not mean there is anything wrong with either party or the relationship. Just this understanding can heal many relationships. Focusing on what we enjoy about each other rather than what is different builds harmony.

Over time I began to make lists of things about Gail that I appreciated. For example, Gail enjoys our home being neat and well-kept. She is always cleaning, painting, or planting something. It is sometimes difficult to get her to stop puttering around the house long enough to ride our horses, play golf, go swimming, watch a movie, or do any of the many other things we enjoy. For years I'd ask myself, "Why is she such a clean freak about our home? Why can't she just let it go for a while and have some fun?" My focus, as directed by the questions I asked myself, was on what I felt was lacking in her. But then something happened that helped me shift my perspective and appreciate this quirk of hers rather than focusing on it as being something wrong.

One night Gail and I along with several friends met for dinner at another couple's home. This couple seemed to have it all. Their home was large, expensive, and in a highly sought-after neighborhood. Their children always looked like they were waiting for a Laura Ashley Kids photographer to snap the catalogue cover photo. The husband and wife were two of the most attractive people you can imagine. He was tall, fit, and rugged, with a square jaw, clear blue eyes, and wavy brown hair. She was tall, blond, and shapely, with a perfect nose and teeth that would make any orthodontist proud.

As we entered their home, I was reminded of comedian George Gobel when he appeared on *The Tonight Show* as Johnny Carson's final guest one evening, following Bob Hope and Dean Martin. Gobel looked at Hope and Martin, both megastars of the day, and joked, "Did you ever get the feeling that the world is a tuxedo and you're a pair of brown shoes?" Well, I felt like a pair of brown shoes in this couple's home.

At one point during the evening, I excused myself and went in search of a restroom. "Down the hall, last door on the left," the strikingly beautiful wife told me. When I reached the end of the hall, I accidentally opened the last door on the *right*—a door that led into the couple's bedroom. I was shocked at what I found. Their room was filthy. I don't mean untidy, I mean filthy. Not only was the bed unmade and the floor festooned with clothes but there were several piles of dog droppings on the floor; the stench was nauseating.

When we first drove up to their home, I found myself asking questions such as "Why don't we live in a neighborhood like this?"—and, I'm somewhat ashamed to admit, "Why doesn't my wife look like her?" (Gail may have asked herself a similar question comparing me to the husband.) Stumbling into their bedroom and seeing how disgusting it was, all I could think was, "Why would I *ever* be upset that my wife is so fastidious about our home? I am one lucky guy! I would not trade my wife and her neatnik ways for the other woman or their seemingly idyllic life."

Incidentally, the couple divorced a year or so later in a bitter dispute that revealed that the pressure of trying to appear so perfect to the outside world had killed their relationship with each other.

In every moment each of us is a different person than we were in the moment preceding or will be in the moment forthcoming. The stream is always flowing, never the same twice as you step into it. We are flowing, growing, and evolving beings and therefore our relationships change as we change. Everyone lives in his or her own reality, which is constantly shifting, ever evolving, and shaped entirely from his or her perspective. Are we asking ourselves questions that evoke appreciation for this transition or that condemn the inevitability of such progress? Are we asking ourselves what we enjoy, appreciate, and hold dear about the other person or are we asking what should go on our laundry list of irritations?

Our life is a journey of exploration and growth. We break through to new levels of expression as we pass through the events of our lives. Our relationships reach new heights if we appreciate the other person in that moment, rather than lamenting how he or she has changed or how we wish he or she would change.

Because each of us is different at any given moment and each of us has a wholly unique perspective, one of the worst things we can do is to disagree about "reality." Arguing over the facts is a waste of time and yet is something people in dissatisfied relationships do on a regular basis.

Never argue about reality.

A while back, my daughter, Lia, then age 12, and I were enjoying a week together at Disney World. A few days into our trip, I called to make dinner reservations at a Disney theme restaurant. Later, as we waited in a line at one of the attractions, Lia asked, "What time is our dinner reservation?"

"Seven," I said.

"You told me it's at six-thirty," she said.

"No, I didn't," I said with a smile. "It's at seven."

"Then why did you tell me six-thirty?" she said, turning around to face me.

"I didn't." My smile began to fade.

"Yes, you did, Dad."

"No, I didn't, buddy."

"Yes, you did. When we were standing on the balcony of our hotel room I asked you what time we were going to eat dinner tonight and you said six-thirty." Her tone of voice was rising.

"No, I didn't." My tone now matching hers.

"Yes, you did."

"No, I didn't."

"You did."

"I didn't."

Et cetera, et cetera, ad infinitum.

We had traveled to the "happiest place on earth," a place built on make-believe, and yet we were getting angry over whose version of reality was accurate. Talk about irony!

QUESTION: In my conversation with my Lia, what was the only important issue?

ANSWER: The correct time for our dinner reservation.

Did it matter whether I had told her incorrectly or if she had simply heard me incorrectly? Not in the least. And yet we found ourselves unwittingly meandering toward an argument over something that was of no importance. Why was this happening? Because Lia was asking herself questions such as:

"Why did Dad tell me a different time than the one he originally told me?"

"What's wrong with him?"

"Why is he getting defensive?"

And I was asking myself questions such as:

"Why does she always have to argue?"

"Who does she think she is, talking back to her father like that?"

"Why doesn't she pay attention to me when I talk to her?"

Listen to people's interactions and you will hear them argue extensively about reality. They try to prove that their version of reality is accurate and that the other person's is wrong. Arguing about reality is a lost cause. Everyone lives in his or her own world, a world that—although it may be constantly shifting because the person him- or herself is changing—the other person feels is the one and only correct reality. For that person, it *is* reality—period. When we attempt to prove our perspective is right and the other person's perspective is wrong, we end up in arguments that are often nothing more than launching points for further hurtful exchanges.

As our "reality" disagreement escalated, Lia and I began to speak more angrily to each other. Luckily, the humor in our arguing over reality while standing in the land of make-believe kicked in for me. I doused the fire before it burned our good time to the ground by saying, "Maybe I said it wrong or perhaps you heard it wrong. Either way, our dinner reservation is at seven."

Lia paused midaccusation and turned back to face the front of the line. "You said six-thirty," she said over her shoulder one last time with fake sarcasm.

"If I did, I'm sorry," I said, my smile returning.

Note that I didn't simply say, "I'm sorry. You were right and I was wrong." Rather, I owned my memory, honored hers, and moved on to what was most important—the two of us having a good time. In any relationship, be it a marriage, work relationship, sibling relationship, casual meeting, or whatever, isn't the bottom line for it to be a pleasant experience? Of course it is. The best to which we can aspire in our personal interactions is that they be joyful.

John Lennon once quipped, "Reality leaves a lot to the imagination." Why? Because reality is a relative concept. You have your reality and the people with whom you share relationships have theirs. They are separate, distinct, and ever changing. Get used to it.

Reality won't even hold up in court. According to a number of research studies, eyewitness accounts make the least credible testimony in a trial. An eyewitness is giving his or her account of what transpired, an account that is tainted by beliefs, moods, prejudices, feelings, emotions, justifications, and many other factors that shade things in one direction or another.

If you've ever been in a traffic accident, you probably know how true this is. Just moments after the accident you and the other person will begin to give your statement about what happened to the police officer only to discover that you have quite different memories of what just occurred. Both of you were present. You're both telling the truth from your perspective. Both of you were eyewitnesses to the same incident. And yet the police officer is left trying to discern whose version of reality is most probable or what combination of the two stories seems most plausible. Truly, reality does leave a lot to the imagination.

> Reality leaves a lot to the imagination.
> —JOHN LENNON

Joseph Campbell said that *reality* is the only word in the English language that should always be written in quotes. Reality is relative to the person speaking about it and to get caught up in an argument over whose version of reality is correct ensures that the current reality, the present moment, will be miserable for both. We live in our own, different worlds but relationships are about our worlds coming together. If we insist that ours is the correct and only world and disregard the legitimacy of the world the other person finds him- or herself in, we are asking for troubled relationships.

One of my favorite things is to sneak away for an afternoon movie. I have found that if I select the film and the time right, I can sometimes be the only one in the theater. I enjoy this most of all. Sitting alone in a large, otherwise empty movie theater makes me feel like a powerful studio executive.

A few years ago, after working several weeks in a row without a break, I slipped out to a local theater. I found a seat in the very center of the auditorium just as the house lights dimmed. As I looked around, I was happy to see that I was the only one present. As the opening credits began, an elderly couple entered. There were nearly 400 empty seats in the theater but the pair chose to sit *directly* behind me.

Now, a little history of my movie-going is required here, a history about which I am none too proud. I used to be the "silence police" at movie theaters. If people talked during a movie, I would not hesitate to give them a dirty look. If they talked again, I would shush them. And if they persisted, I'm embarrassed to admit, I would get the manager. I'm not proud of this. But the truly interesting thing is that as I became less consumed by listening to see who was breaking my "silence ban," I found that fewer and fewer people were doing so. I was attracting rude people by the chip I carried on my shoulders.

The elderly couple who had chosen to sit directly behind me that day began to talk—loudly. From the first scene until the closing credits, they talked. Not only did they talk, they did so in full voice. Several times I thought about shushing them. I even thought about going to the manager. "That's the old me," I told myself. "I can still enjoy the movie without having to get them in trouble or acting angrily toward them." If their talking became too distracting, I reasoned, I could always move to another part of the theater. With that awareness, I was able to mentally block out their dialogue and enjoy the film.

At the end of the movie, I rose to leave and, for the first time, took a good look at the two of them. They were quite elderly. As the gentleman slowly stood, pulling himself up on the back of my seat, I could see his hearing aids. He turned to his date, who was every bit his age, and helped her as she rose on unsteady legs. As she stood, she extended a telescoping white cane that was red near the tip. A rush of understanding flooded my mind as I thought back to their comments during the film.

In my world, two rude people who had no concept of movie protocol had, of all the seats in the theater, chosen to sit down right behind me. My reality had been that they had yakked inanely about things that were self-evident on the screen. My reality was that I was somehow enlightened or spiritually superior because I had not complained about two very discourteous individuals who deserved to be seriously dressed down for their behavior. "At their age," I'd reasoned, "they should have better manners!"

That had been my reality. As I looked at them now, I saw another, very different reality. I caught a glimpse of their world and it stopped my critical thoughts short. I saw him with his hearing aids and her with her cane for the sight-impaired. I realized that the talking they had been engaging in was not mindless chatter but helpful exposition. She was almost completely blind and he was telling her what she could not see, whereas he was nearly deaf and she was repeating what he could not hear.

I don't remember the movie I saw that day, but I will never forget the image of this loving couple as they shuffled slowly out of the theater, arm in arm, smiling all the while.

The Buddha taught that the origin of suffering is attachment. Each of us lives in our own world. "Our world" is our creation and therefore something to which we may be doggedly attached. Outwardly it may look exactly like the world shared by others, but ours is unique, for it has attached to it the meaning and context that we have created in our minds. Our world is an alignment of our own thoughts into a coherent narrative. It seems real but is in actuality a story; a tale, an allegory, a complete fabrication.

To illustrate the impact of our unique worlds on our relationships, imagine a comfortable, pristine podlike room floating through space. It's warm and inviting. It is well lit and roomy. This floating pod represents a potential "relation-ship." At some point you and someone else find yourselves together in this pod/"relation-ship." The catalyst for your being transported into this floating environ may be anything that occasions you to meet. You may be standing next to each other at a Laundromat, you may find yourselves sitting in close proximity in a class, you may find yourselves working together, or you may be introduced by a mutual friend. Whatever brings you together, both of you are now transported into this neutral pod with its bare white walls. Your time there may be just seconds or the rest of your lives.

> Our world is an alignment of our own thoughts into a coherent narrative; it seems real but it is in actuality a story, a tale, an allegory, a complete fabrication.

Both of you have brought with you memories of your "home planets"—your unique worlds. Moreover, each of you has brought with you a thick portfolio of photographs that represent things you like and things you dislike. As you spend time together in this pod, you both begin to decorate it with the photographs based on what you experience and perceive about each another. If you discover something you like about the other person, you tack up an image that makes you feel happy, comfortable, or safe. If you experience the other person as being discourteous or spiteful, you put up a picture that represents being treated rudely, being angry, or being threatened. Up and down the once bare walls you both scamper in the "relation-ship." All these images you are slapping up evoke emotions. Further, as the other person puts up an image, you find yourself putting up images that reflect the content of the other person's posted pictures. The images begin to totally fill the walls of the pod and you find yourself feeling and reacting not so much to the other person as to the images you are seeing.

Over time, your bond with the other person begins to reflect the images on the walls rather than the other way around. You no longer see the other person; you see the images you have pasted up and the images the other person has posted. You are no longer two wonderful and unique individuals coming together in a pristine environment; you are now two automatons reacting to the stimuli around you. The "relation-ship" is on autopilot. If the images that you have tacked up are joyous, trusting, and harmonious, then you are gliding along smoothly and enjoying the ride. If the images are critical, distrustful, and combative, you find yourself on a very uncomfortable and bumpy trip.

If the trip is smooth, wonderful; but what can you do if the ride is rough, bouncing through space and jarring your bones? One of the best things you can do is understand that what is happening is a result of the pictures you have posted and to which you continually but unconsciously refer. Both you and the other person are reacting to the images you have placed on the walls.

When someone is upset with you, there is something very freeing in simply saying to yourself, "That's just a picture he's hung up in our relationship." Saying this or "That's just a picture she has hung in her mind" to yourself when someone is angry dissipates defensiveness and the need to hang a similarly negative picture about the other person. It depersonalizes the experience. This is powerful.

Further, you can choose to be proactive rather than reactive, which is always best. If someone is upset with you and has hung a disparaging picture of you in your "relation-ship" pod, respond by hanging an understanding picture of that person. Post an image that reflects an understanding of the difficulties that person may be or may have been facing that caused him or her to act that way.

If you can stop the picture-posting competition by not posting a negative image or, better yet, by posting one that causes you to act in a caring way toward the other person, you can smooth out the voyage of your relationship. Even if the other person continues to slap up one negative picture after another, if you can refuse to respond in kind, you will find a sense of peace and, in time, positively transform the relationship.

Have you noticed that some hotels not only hang pictures in their rooms but screw them into the walls? Well, it is likely that you not only have posted pictures in all of your "relation-ships" but in many of them you have screwed these images securely into the walls. If these are images that evoke good feelings about the other person, then you are experiencing the positive nature of these posts. If, however, they are images that serve as reminders to hold a grudge, you may want to consider removing them or, better yet, replacing them. Constantly looking at negative, painful, and hurtful images only serves to compound your pain and discomfort in the relationship.

> Carefully select the pictures you hang in your "relation-ship."

If something has transpired between the two of you that causes you to feel angry or upset, it is incumbent upon *you* to release it. This is the essence of forgiveness. *Forgiveness* is defined as "to release resentment." It is an internal process. It is letting go of your energy about what has happened. You need not even say anything to the other person; you remove the picture from *your* mind.

A step toward forgiving someone is to ask yourself what good has come as a result of the challenging incident. If enough time has not elapsed for a gift to be revealed and if the pain is still raw, then ask what the experience has given you in the form of growth or direction for your life and begin to give thanks for that.

Your mind will probably revolt as you begin this process. It is not easy but forgiveness is crucial for your happiness and for success in relationships.

Clean up the past by forgiving. Many a current relationship has gone south because one of the people in the relationship has held resentments against someone in a previous relationship and projected those resentments onto their current partner. Unscrew the image from the wall and release it; let it go; burn it. Relinquish your resentment.

> Forgiveness is crucial for your happiness and for success in relationships.

Think of the word *resentment* as "re-sendment." When you hold resentments you are sending the negative energy back to yourself. Being unwilling to forgive is like throwing a boomerang covered in filth that gathers more filth during its flight and returns for you to catch. When you cling to resentment, it does not hurt the other person, it hurts you.

A family I know once found an abandoned Siamese kitten. They already had a cat and were not looking for another pet but something about this particular kitten resonated with them and they welcomed her into their home. They asked their two-year-old daughter what to name the cuddly kitten and she said, "Marvel." Marvel became a much-loved part of the family.

Marvel was curious and playful, as kittens are. She was primarily an inside cat, although she ventured out of doors on rare occasions, scampering back to the safety of home whenever she felt threatened or afraid. The family loved and doted on Marvel and she returned their affection, sleeping next to the young girl's head or resting for hours on the mother's chest gently kneading her sweater.

The man who lived directly across the street had pets as well—two large, energetic Dobermans. The dogs lived in a fenced-in portion of the neighbor's yard but spent time in his garage every day. As they were moved from the yard to the garage each day they were at liberty for a few moments without a leash or any other restraint.

One day the dogs caught a glimpse of Marvel, who was sitting quietly on the front steps meticulously licking each of her paws clean. In a flash the dogs ran across the street, their barks sending Marvel into a panic. In her mad rush to get away from the two marauding monsters she ran as fast as she could around the back of the house and leaped up on the back deck. The woman managed to sweep Marvel up into the safety of her arms just as the Dobermans crested the stairs to attack.

Embarrassed, the neighbor came to retrieve his dogs and pulled them one by one back to the confines of the garage. Having rescued Marvel just seconds before the dogs attacked, the woman was shaking with fear and rage. She yelled over at the neighbor, "Keep those damn dogs under control or you're going to have a vet bill to pay." Shivering, she held Marvel close as she walked back into their home.

Several weeks later, the woman awoke to what she describes as "a sickening sound." Putting on her glasses, she raced to the window and saw the two dogs playing tug-of-war with Marvel's body. Blood and fur flew in every direction as Marvel hissed and clawed in a vain effort to stave off the assault. Filled with rage and adrenaline, the woman rushed into the fray, driving the Dobermans away. Sobbing, she cradled Marvel's savagely wounded body and ran to her car to take Marvel to the veterinarian. The owner of the Dobermans, having once again corralled the dogs, stood in shocked silence as he watched the woman's car disappear down the street.

"There was nothing the vet could do," the woman told me. "We had Marvel put down." For days the family grieved her passing. A note from the Dobermans' owner appeared in their mailbox: "I'm sorry you had to put your cat to sleep. I will pay the vet bill." The neighbor's apology took a little of the sting out of the experience and his promise to pay the vet bill seemed only fair.

The woman walked across the street to deliver the $475 veterinarian's bill. She remembers, "I took him the bill and he scoffed at it. I was furious; I lost my temper and we had words. He blamed the fact that Marvel was outside for the dogs chasing her. Before I knew it we were yelling at each other. I finally stormed off."

In time, the vet's office called to say the bill had not been paid but the woman was still so angry she could not face her neighbor again. "We just paid the bill," she said. "It wasn't worth talking to him again.

"For a year and a half there was a frozen silence between me and this man who lived less than a stone's throw across the street," the woman said. "I found myself looking outside to make sure I wouldn't have to face him when I left the house. If we did happen to be outdoors at the same time, we both averted our eyes so as not to look at each other. I felt rotten, but I also felt justified in my anger. I tried putting the whole experience out of my mind but couldn't. The anger just bubbled inside me. I found myself being short-tempered with husband and my son."

> The one who gives is the one who has the most control.
>
> —CHRISTINE MADOR

During the Fourth of July weekend eighteen months after Marvel's death, the woman had a breakthrough. "I had an intense feeling that I needed to let this go. I needed to stop punishing him because I was punishing myself; every time I looked at this guy I was thinking about Marvel's death." Not sure of what to do next, she did what came to her naturally—she baked a batch of her famous chocolate chip cookies and put them in a large bowl. She tied a cheerful bow around the bowl and trudged slowly across the street to where the neighbor was gardening.

"As was now our custom," she said, "my neighbor looked away

when he saw me. As I approached him a song kept running through my head. The song was 'Say What You Need to Say' by John Mayer. It goes: 'Walking like a one-man army, fighting with the shadows in your head, living out the same old moment, knowing you'd be better off instead, if you could only say what you need to say.' "

Looking like a small rabbit cornered with nowhere to run, the man finally raised his eyes. The woman smiled and handed him the gift. She had included a card with the cookies that read, *Happy Fourth of July. I'm sorry the memory of Marvel's death has kept me from being neighborly to you.*

"At first he looked stunned," she told me. "Then he looked so relieved; I'm sure it had been eating him up inside, too." The woman turned and glided back across the street. The incident was now put to rest. She had let it go once and for all and it no longer tormented her. Marvel now rested in peace.

"Since then, we've been very cordial. We say, 'Hi, how are you doing?' or 'Nice day today, isn't it?' He's never going to be my best friend but I don't have to hate him, and I don't." The woman released her resentment. It is no longer boomeranging back her way with painful memories of her beloved cat.

Best-selling author Lawana Blackwell wrote, "Forgiveness is almost a selfish act because of its immense benefits to the one who forgives." We all have people we need to forgive. You will know that you are "resending" resentments whenever you bring someone to mind or hear their name and find yourself feeling anger, frustration, or pain. These emotions exist in the same place as all of your relationships—your mind—and it is here that you can now free yourself from the pain of your resentment. You are carrying the pain. You are exhuming the struggle. You are eating away at your own soul with these negative thoughts and feelings. You are hurting yourself, not the other person. Famed nineteenth-century American clergyman Harry Emerson Fosdick said, "Hating people is like burning down your own house to get rid of a rat." You need to stop burning down your emotional and spiritual house; you need to forgive.

A good method for forgiveness is to sit quietly and comfortably with your eyes closed. Begin to breathe deeply, allowing your stomach—not your chest—to expand as you inhale and contract as you exhale. As you do this, imagine you are seated front row center in a large, opulent theater, a classic venue with ornate decorations and a grand chandelier suspended above the main seating area. You are alone in this large theater and feel a sense of detachment, a sense of bliss. Over and over breathe until you feel you truly are seated in such a grand theater. Gaze at the enormous red velvet drapes that adorn the stage before you. The house lights begin to dim, replaced by a lone spotlight casting a large circle of light on the center of the luxurious curtains.

Sit for a moment staring at the circle of light and take several more deep breaths. Then call to mind a person with whom you are having a challenge. It is best not to begin with someone you feel has seriously harmed you or against whom you bear a strong and long-standing resentment. Begin with someone who just bugs you a little. When it comes to forgiveness, just as in life, you must crawl before you can walk.

When you are ready, imagine this person stepping forward onto the stage through the drapes into this bright spotlight. The person is well dressed but comfortable, smiling and content, holding a small wooden-framed chalkboard that is blank. Smiling, you say:

> [PERSON'S NAME], I now release all resentment I have held against you. I welcome you into the bright light of a new day and see you with a clean slate. I celebrate the things you have taught me and give thanks for the gift you are in my life.

Then begin to applaud this person as he or she smiles graciously. When you feel complete with this part of the exercise, invite the person to come and sit next to you.

Having successfully forgiven this person, repeat the process with someone else. Now, however, you have a momentum of forgiveness, as the person who was once your enemy now sits at your side as a caring and supportive ally.

I once spent a weekend doing this very exercise. It was a powerful and transformative experience as I called to mind person after person. I was surprised how many people I had negative energy toward. I discovered that there were some people I was not ready to forgive. If I could not invite them to sit next to me as a true friend and spiritual guide, I simply apologized, told them I was not ready, and asked them to wait in the greenroom backstage as I continued the visualization, calling others forward one by one. After a while, and with more new allies in the seats surrounding me offering support and encouragement, I would invite them back and try to forgive again. If I was still not yet ready, I asked them to return again to the greenroom until I was able to give them another try.

It is important as you do this not to judge yourself for your inability to forgive some people. This is a process of cleaning up an attic full of emotional cobwebs and it cannot and should not be rushed. It takes time but it is time that yields incredible freedom.

Forgiving is "for giving." It is a gift you give yourself.

James Arthur Ray has said that you will know you have truly forgiven someone when you can look beyond the sting of the experience and say with sincerity, "Thank you for giving me this experience." Enrique Gutierrez, the Cuban man I mentioned in the introduction who was beaten and imprisoned by the Castro regime, is now a shining example of peace thanks to his willingness to forgive his tormentors. The pain they inflicted on him was very real but he has chosen not to keep it alive by inflicting the memory of it on himself today. He has released it. Unfortunately, he has a family member who received similar treatment who suffers emotional pain some twenty years later because he has been unwilling to let go of what happened to him. He continues to hold resentments today for what happened decades ago. The cumulative total of reliving his vile treatment has been more painful than the actual experience.

Don't hang pictures in your "relation-ship" that you don't want to influence the course of the relationship. When a negative image passes through your mind about someone, let it keep passing. Don't tack it to the wall. And if the other person acts in a way that seems to say he or she is angry or resentful toward you, remind yourself, "Oh, yes, that's a picture that person has hung about me. That's all it is. It's that person's reality, not mine."

> You will know you have truly forgiven when you can look beyond the sting of the experience and say with sincerity, "Thank you for giving me this experience."

You may be thinking, "If I did that, I'd just be faking it. I want to be real in my relationships and that wouldn't be true." Remember that truth, as it relates to events, is a relative perspective. According to Bible historians, the oldest surviving scrap of New Testament manuscript is a tattered fragment containing only John 18:38. In this passage, Pilate poses to Jesus the central theme of this chapter when he asks simply, "What is truth?" How ironic and profound that the oldest piece of Christian writing questions how one can get hold of declarative, undeniable, unquestioned truth when there is no such thing, only the perspective from a person's unique world.

In the blockbuster movie *The Matrix,* Morpheus, played by Laurence Fishburne, is asked by Neo, played by Keanu Reeves, if the realm in which they find themselves is real. Morpheus responds, "What is *real*? How do you define *real*? If you are talking about what you can feel, what you can smell, taste, and see, then *real* is simply electrical signals interpreted by your brain."

Every experience is interpreted by our brains and it is during this interpretation process that differences occur, differences that can become problems if we attempt to declare that only our version is "real."

You may think that we could solve a lot of conflicts if our minds were like computers—logical and dispassionate, devoid of personalities and agendas. Well, maybe not.

Decades ago, one of the earliest language interpretation computers was given a task. It was asked to translate the common English idiom "Out of sight, out of mind" from the English language to Spanish, then to German, then to French, and finally back to English. After complying with the request, the computer, which is a neutral, logical machine and not an emotional human with a personal history, perspective, or agenda, brought back a translation that, although literal, carried a very different meaning from the original words. "Out of sight, out of mind" came back as "Invisible, insane."

When it comes to relationships—indeed, when it comes to life—there is no reality, only perspective. Don't get caught up in arguing about reality; simply agree that you have different perspectives and/or memories and move on. Your need to be right encourages you to fight for your version of reality, but when you do, the ensuing argument can weaken the foundation of the relationship. Even if you win—that is, you get the other person to agree that your description of what happened is accurate—you feel only the elation of victory over the other person, not the true peace of mastering yourself. Winning over another only prepares you to fight the next time—and it ensures there *will* be a next time—whereas refusing to fight makes you less likely to be attacked again.

Now, if you are in a position of authority (for example, if you are a parent or an employer), when it comes to matters of quantifiable performance your version of reality wins. You get to dictate—but make certain you are a benevolent dictator. In these situations, someone must be the one to set the standard for acceptable levels of performance and hold the others to it. If you are the leader, that someone is you. It is important that you clearly convey your expectations to the other people and make sure they understand. Don't assume they know what you expect. It is up to you to communicate your expectations.

> The ultimate test of a relationship is to disagree but hold hands.
> —ALEXANDER PENNEY

If an employee is consistently late, you could get bogged down arguing over whose watch has the correct time. Communicate that when it comes to the time work begins, your clock is the official measure and the employee must abide by it. If not, that's fine—but that employee won't be working with you and your company.

Teenagers may feel their room is clean but you may disagree. If this is the case, you have a communication problem. Work with them to get the room to a level you find acceptable. Once this is done, agree on what the reality for "clean room" looks like (e.g., no clothes on the floor, bed neatly made, games and other items put in proper places, etc.). From that point forward, the room is clean only when it is at this level.

I know of a couple who ran into this issue with their teenage son. They would ask him to clean his room and he would emerge a half hour or so later to announce that the room was clean and then leave to be with friends. Surveying the results, the parents found the room was, in their opinion, definitely *not* clean. For months they yelled at the boy and threatened him. The parents found that complaining about his not cleaning his room properly only made him less likely to keep it tidy. They felt he was being disrespectful; he felt they were harassing him.

In time, the parents realized that they had a clash of realities.

Their son wasn't being disrespectful. He sincerely felt the room was up to standard—*his* standard. They decided to help him understand *their* standard. First they showed him their room and asked, "What do you notice about the cleanliness of our room as compared to yours?"

"Well," he said, "the bed is made and there aren't any wrinkles in it. The dresser doesn't have much stuff on it. And there aren't any clothes or dishes around."

"Exactly," the mom said. "Now let's go see how this compares with your room." They then let the teenager point out the differences. They allowed him to express what was different about his room because if they did, it might have sounded like more complaining. Because he had viewed his parents' room as a frame of reference, the dissimilarities in tidiness were readily apparent.

Then the parents said, "Let us help you get your room up to the same level as ours," and the three set about cleaning the room. When they finished, the father said, "Okay, the room is clean. What does this look like? What does it mean to have a clean room?" They listened as their son answered, and when all agreed, the parents said, "Great. When we say, 'Please clean your room,' if it doesn't look like this, it's not clean. And that means you can't go out and be with your friends, get on your computer, text friends, or do anything else until it's at this level of orderliness. You stay with the task until it's this clean, understood?" The teen agreed and they have not had an issue since.

Every problem is a communication problem. If you look deeply, you will find that nearly all conflict is based on a misunderstanding that can be resolved through clear communication. It is incumbent upon the person communicating to deliver the message in such a way that it is received. Complaining that the other person "doesn't listen" or "doesn't get it" removes the communicating person from the responsibility of successfully conveying the message. Further, as we'll discuss later, it excuses the person hearing the message because he or she has been defined as "a person who does not listen" and acts accordingly. Successful communication is about owning your experience of what happened rather than trying to press the other person to agree that your version is the only accurate one. Successful communication comes from using the word *I* a lot more than the word *you*.

A successful communicator says, "*I* felt angry." Owning the experience in this manner, the speaker opens doors of communication. A poor communicator says, "*You* made me angry." This slams shut the doors of communication because the other person feels attacked and may react with a counterattack. Using "I" statements means the person owns the experience as just that: his or her experience. "You" statements imply that the speaker is a victim focusing blame for his or her upset on the other person.

A family therapist once shared with me a powerful communication technique, and according to another therapist I interviewed, this method has been used successfully by counselors for decades. It is a three-step process where one person makes a statement, the other person paraphrases back what he or she has heard the speaker say, and the first person either agrees that the listener has accurately understood or not. If the speaker agrees that the listener's understanding is accurate, the two switch roles. If two people are having trouble communicating, this can be a very effective way to reach clarity and understanding.

I have created a mnemonic device to help you remember the three steps, with the words describing each step all rhyming with the letter *A*. Remember, successful relationships always get an A in communication.

SAY   One person says something—for example, "I want us to spend more quality time together. We both work late and then sit and watch television. I'm just not feeling close to you."

REPLAY   The other person listens without comment. When the speaker is finished, the listener paraphrases back what was heard to verify that he or she has accurately understood— for example, "What I'm hearing you say is that you want us to spend more time together without the distraction of television."

OKAY   The listener then asks for agreement: "Do I understand you correctly?" or "Is that right?" If the speaker gives the okay that he or she was indeed understood, it is then the listener's turn to make a statement.

The person who previously spoke now listens, replays the comment back to clarify understanding, and then asks if he or she has understood correctly. If the speaker does not give the okay, the speaker is asked to repeat the statement, and the process is repeated.

> I know you think you understand what you thought I said, but I'm not sure that what you heard is exactly what I meant.
>
> —CLASSIC QUOTE, PARAPHRASED

Back and forth the discourse flows as each person takes a turn speaking and the other person listens, paraphrases, and seeks verification. It can feel halting and stilted at first but it prevents the anger and frustration that can erupt when one or both parties are misunderstood.

A newly married couple came to me for counseling. They were very upset. The wife said, "We seem to talk *at* each other rather than talking *with* each other—we're not communicating." She said that their discussions regularly broke down into heated arguments.

I suggested they try this technique and the husband later reported, "It wasn't easy to stop and put this framework around our conversations. But we agreed that *every time* either of us felt ourselves becoming upset we would do this. It was cumbersome at first but it has become a habit and we're communicating wonderfully."

His wife added, "Even if we don't say, 'Let's use the three steps,' either one of us can simply replay and ask if we understood correctly anything the other person says. If he says something, I can simply say, 'What I'm hearing you say is . . . ; is that correct?' If he says I'm not getting his point, I ask him to repeat and then I paraphrase again until he okays my understanding. This opens us up to understanding what the other person said rather than what we thought we heard."

All of us have our own unique perspective. All of us live in our own world. We can get caught up in a disagreement about the context of another person's perspective or we can seek to understand the underlying content. It is our choice. By seeking to understand, we can avoid hanging hurtful and destructive pictures in our relationship.

I was recently addressing a large group of teachers and school psychologists on the concept of how we create our lives through our thoughts. I explained that we can choose to think thoughts that make us happy or unhappy. Neither is incorrect but each is causative. Each has a result that becomes our reality. Happy thoughts yield happy attitudes, which create happy experiences. Unhappy thoughts yield an unhappy demeanor and result in unhappy experiences. A woman in the front row raised her hand. "I don't like people who are happy all the time," she said. "They are faking it!"

I thought a moment before responding. With her clenched jaw and intense glare, she looked ready for me to take issue with her perspective—to challenge her reality. Instead, I smiled and said, "I agree." She looked at me quizzically. "From your point of view," I said, "people who are happy all the time are faking it." She looked like she was waiting for the other shoe to drop, and after a moment of silence I let it fall. "From my perspective," I said, "people who are miserable all the time are also faking it. Perhaps everyone is faking it. If that's the case, I think I'll choose to fake it in a way that positively energizes me and those around me."

I could have taken issue with what she said. I could have quoted studies from the emerging field of positive psychology in an attempt to prove her wrong. But I saw no need for our distinct worlds to collide. They could coexist compatibly. My world can be populated by people who are happy most of the time—and it is. Hers will be a reflection of the thoughts she holds in her mind.

One of my favorite movies was the original *Planet of the Apes* starring Charlton Heston, Kim Hunter, and Roddy McDowall. I recently saw a documentary on this film, which was quite a phenomenon in its day. The producers of the movie made a decision to do everything they could to create the illusion that the story was actually set on a planet with humanlike apes. A commitment was made early in production that no masks would be used on any of the actors. Regardless of how remote the shot or how brief the appearance, each extra would have the same full prosthetic makeup worn by the lead actors.

In the documentary, McDowall explained that making other movies in Hollywood at this time was difficult because nearly every makeup artist in the industry was brought in to work on *Planet of the Apes.* An assembly line was created whereby the actors went from chair to chair having latex appliances, makeup, and hair applied to their faces. It took several hours to complete the process on each actor but the assembly-line approach kept the makeup process to just six to eight hours for all the actors and extras.

McDowall noticed that as they were waiting to be transformed into apes, the actors tended to hang around together based on ethnicity. The white actors would hang out with the white actors, the black actors hung out together, the Asian actors congregated with the other Asian actors, and the Latino actors clustered with the Latino actors. As they went through the makeup process, each of the extras came out randomly as either a gorilla, an orangutan, or a chimpanzee.

The interesting thing McDowall noted was that after they were transformed into apes, the actors no longer congregated by race. Instead, the gorillas hung around with the gorillas, the orangutans with the orangutans, and the chimpanzees with the chimpanzees.

People are drawn to people they perceive to be like them. If our realities—our worlds—are created by images of happy, harmonious, and supportive people, these people will show up for us. If our worlds are dark, dangerous places, we will experience people who reinforce this reality. Our worlds are a creation of the questions we ask ourselves and the pictures we hang in our minds.

Willa Cather wrote, "In reality, of course, life rushes from within, not from without." Take a look at your relationships and own your ability to transform them. Ask questions that build bridges; hang pictures that support harmony. Forgive others for their transgressions and honor your unique world and the world in which the other person lives.

Opening Up

1. When you are with someone and you sense discord ask yourself, "How are we able to exist and perform in a harmonious and agreeable way?" Let this question be a mantra that repeats in your mind.

2. Whenever you find yourself disagreeing over reality, simply say to the other person, "I honor that as your perspective," and let it go. Repeat as necessary.

3. Do a mental inventory of the people in your life, both currently and in your past. As you think of them, check in with yourself to see if you have any angry or unsettled feelings. Then spend some time performing the forgiveness exercise detailed in this chapter.

4. Ask someone to rehearse the "Say, Replay, Okay" technique. Take turns and work through the three steps. Then commit to trying this the next time you are in a confrontation with someone. Let the other person speak, paraphrase back, and ask if you are correct, "What I'm hearing you say is . . . ," and then ask, "Is that correct?" When and only when the other person agrees you are correct, make your statement.

CHAPTER 3

Getting Your Needs Met

Man is an animal which, alone among the animals, refuses to be satisfied by the fulfillment of animal desires.
— ALEXANDER GRAHAM BELL

We all have needs we want fulfilled. Beyond basic human needs for food, water, shelter, and sex, human beings possess limitless desires. Many relationships experience challenges because the people within them complain to and about each other in an attempt to get these needs met. Rather than improving things, complaints often keep them mired in their current problems and perpetuate their frustration.

In "A Descriptive Taxonomy of Couples' Complaint Interactions," Dr. J. K. Alberts wrote, "Negative communication, such as complaining, can be an important factor in a couple's relational satisfaction." Alberts further stated, as mentioned in the introduction to this book, "Diverse research indicates that negativity and negative communication are positively correlated with relational dissatisfaction."

TRANSLATION: People who are in relationships where there is a lot of complaining tend to be less happy in those relationships.

In *Family Communication,* authors Chris Segrin and Jeanne Flora note, "It is not particularly surprising that distressed couples exhibit negativity during their interactions and that these interactions are the source of a lot of negative emotions. Undoubtedly, the negative communication behaviors and negative emotions displayed in these interactions are causally related."

TRANSLATION: Complaining in relationships may begin as a result of one or both people being dissatisfied in the relationship and attempting to get their needs met. Soon, however, the complaining itself becomes the cause of dissatisfaction and escalates it. A "Dissatisfaction → Complaint" loop is created, in which dissatisfaction leads to a complaint, which leads to dissatisfaction, which leads to another complaint, which causes more dissatisfaction, and on it goes.

A 1988 study by Lowell J. Krokoff, John M. Gottman, and Anup K. Roy found that "decreasing negative affect has more effect on improving couple's marital happiness than increasing positive affect."

TRANSLATION: Stopping the negativity of complaining does more to improve relationships than does adding positive aspects to the relationship. In other words, it's more beneficial to the relationship to send kind words than to send flowers.

Dissatisfaction   Complaint

In an attempt to get our needs met in relationships, people tend to complain about what they are experiencing rather than express what they desire. And yet these studies confirm that the acid that erodes the foundations of most relationships is complaining.

Complaining *to* another person lowers the overall energy of the relationship. Complaining *about* the other person makes him or her feel less valued by you and can drive a wedge into the relationship. Further, when you negatively describe a person by complaining about him or her, the person integrates this description and tends to react accordingly by perpetuating the behavior you are complaining about. Best-selling author Dr. Thomas Stanley put it this way: "Labels often have a way of activating behaviors that are congruent with designations." Just as the women who said "all men are dogs" perpetuated the men in their lives acting like dogs, when you complain to someone about his or her behavior, the person is *more,* not less, likely to continue that behavior.

What is complaining? The dictionary defines *complain* as "to express grief, pain, or discontent." As concise as this definition is, it still may leave us questioning whether what we are saying is a complaint or a statement of fact. My own definition of a complaint is "an energetic statement focused on the problem at hand rather than the resolution sought."

Dr. Robin Kowalski of Clemson University wrote, "Whether or not the particular statement reflects a complaint depends on whether the speaker is experiencing an internal dissatisfaction."

For a statement to be a complaint there must be an internal dissatisfaction, an upset, or negative energy behind the comment.

"It's hot today" is a statement of fact. It is not a complaint. "It's *so* hot today!" is a complaint. The statement implies that the person making the second comment feels that it should not be as warm as it is and has negative feelings about it being so.

> A complaint is an energetic statement focused on the problem at hand rather than the resolution sought.

"You left your socks on the floor" is a statement of fact. "You always leave your damn socks on the floor" is a complaint. It carries negative energy. Statements of fact are neutral; complaints are laced with negative energy. The words can be identical; it's the underlying energy that distinguishes a complaint from a statement of fact. In the examples above, I added words ("so," "always," and "damn") because they convey the negative energy behind those statements.

In most cases, the negative energy surrounding a complaint conveys a belief that the primary purpose of the situation is to affront or annoy the person expressing the complaint. The implied emotion is "How dare you [or God, or the universe, or the weather, or whatever] do this to me?"

We tend to take events and other people's actions personally. Why is this? Why do we feel as if everything is about us? Because all of us are the emperors or empresses of our own private worlds; therefore, to us, all events and activities *are* about us. Each of us lives in our own reality, a world of our creation, a world that emanates from our inner being. Because each of us is the center of our world, when we experience something we do not like, we take it as a personal slight. We'll talk more about the reasons we take things personally later and how we can avoid doing so. For now, understand that most complaints have a negative emotion attached with the underlying belief that whatever is happening is "being done to me."

If complaining is so damaging to our relationships, you may wonder why we complain. Why do we engage in something that has been shown in a great number of research studies to be the single most destructive thing we can do in our relationships? What would motivate us to engage in an activity that increases discord, perpetuates negative interactions, reinforces irritating behavior, escalates arguments, and drives a wedge between us and another person?

People complain for the same reason that a baby cries: they are dissatisfied with something and lack the verbal skills to get their needs met without resorting to statements that are charged with negativity. Because people consider their version of reality to be the correct and only one, then whatever happens does indeed happen *to them,* and they cry out in an attempt to bring about change. Most people don't understand that they have a much better chance of getting what they desire if they phrase their requests in positive rather than negative ways. If our attempts to get our needs met are phrased in a negative, complaining manner ("You always do this"), the situation tends to perpetuate itself. If phrased in a positive way ("I would like this instead"), the situation tends to get resolved.

> If our attempts to get our needs met are phrased in a negative, complaining manner ("You always do this"), the situation tends to perpetuate itself. If phrased in a positive way ("I would like this instead"), the situation tends to get resolved.

I was recently staying at one of the finest hotels in Denver, Colorado. This hotel is widely celebrated for its splendor, amenities, and guest services, and has earned a number of distinctions and accolades.

I checked into my room, unpacked, and then went down to take a walk around the city. I later went back to my room, changed clothes, and went down to the hotel gym for a refreshing workout. Returning to my room again, I showered, changed, and went downstairs for dinner. When I returned around eight o'clock I heard a rhythmic noise coming from the other side of the wall—a loud noise that I had not heard earlier that day: *whoom . . . squeak . . . whoom . . . squeak . . .*

No, the noise was not what you are thinking. It just so happened that my room was on the sixth floor of this hotel and the building that abutted the hotel was five stories high. There was an enormous, rusty exhaust fan atop the building next door and as it spun—*whoom*—it hit a rusty spot on its frame and gave out a shrill squeak. During previous times in my room that day I had not heard the noise because the fan had been still. It was now operating and making quite a racket.

Because people know me as the "Complaint Free guy" you might wonder how I handled this situation. Simple: I went downstairs and informed the people at the front desk. "You're probably not aware of this," I said, "but there is a fan on top of the building next door, just outside my window, that needs lubricating and it's making a loud noise. I'm supposed to deliver a speech in the morning and need a good night's sleep. Would you mind moving me to another room?" They not only gave me another room, they upgraded me to a beautiful two-level suite.

I was not satisfied being in a noisy room. I wanted a change in the situation. Rather than go to the front desk with a chip on my shoulder, bellowing, "How dare you do this to me?" I realized that surely the management of this fine hotel must not be aware of the squeaky exhaust fan. So I spoke to them in a way that informed them. "You are probably not aware of this . . . ," I began.

> "You are probably not aware of this . . ."

"You are probably not aware of this" is a magic phrase when sharing your needs with someone. It allows you to express your dissatisfaction without making your comments personal. It acknowledges your understanding that the other person's behavior is probably not intended to upset you.

A few weeks ago I was in a movie theater and a woman in front of me kept texting during the movie. Her phone was silent and she was not making any noise, but every time she held up her phone to type or read a text message the light from the phone's screen shone into my eyes. I tapped her shoulder and said, "You're probably not aware of this, but when you hold your phone up like that the light from the screen is distracting. Would you mind not texting during the movie?" She was so surprised by what I said that she jumped a little in her seat. She really was not aware that her texting was bothering anyone. She apologized and switched off her phone.

Like a baby who cries because it lacks the verbal skills to get its needs satisfied, I could have approached the management of the Denver hotel and said, "What the hell is wrong with this place? I thought you were supposed to be one of the finest hotels in Denver!" ("Wahhhhh!" cried the baby.) I could have said to the woman in the theater, "Hey, how about not holding your stupid phone up so that it glares in my face?" ("Wahhhhhh!") But in both cases this would have made them less, not more, likely to comply with my wishes.

If you say, "You're probably not aware of this . . . ," and follow up by explaining how you perceive the situation, most people will hear what you have to say and respond favorably. For this to work, though, it must be done without negative energy, without blame or fault-finding. It should not be "You're probably not aware of this, but your mangy dog is digging up my flower beds and if it happens again I'm going to call the pound." Speaking this way causes people to want to defend themselves; they will dig their heels in and not respond favorably. The words you use must be genuinely intended to inform the other person and must be delivered without rancor or resentment.

In your world, there is an issue, a dissatisfaction. In their world, chances are there is none and they are truly unaware of your unmet need. You are trying to bridge the gap between your two realities and your words should have the impact of a dove landing gently on a tree limb rather than a brick crashing through a window.

"If he loved me, he'd know what I want," a woman recently said to me regarding her husband.

I explained that love does not impart psychic ability. "And," I went on, "the fact that he loves you does not excuse you from taking responsibility for getting your own needs met. Obtaining what you need is your responsibility, not his."

In most cases, when you make the other person aware, he or she will provide what you seek. Most people are friendly, helpful, genial, agreeable, giving, supportive, and willing to please. If, however, saying "You are probably not aware of this . . ." doesn't resolve the situation, then you may need to resort to one of the most powerful activity human beings can engage in—an activity many are hesitant to try. This activity opens doors, loosens purse strings, and paves the way for our desires. The activity is . . . *asking.*

The Denver hotel moved me to another room because I asked. The woman in the theater turned off her phone because I asked. People will do things for you if you ask.

> He who asks is a
> fool for five minutes,
> but he who does
> not ask remains a
> fool forever.
> —CHINESE PROVERB

If this is so, why are we hesitant to ask? Because we fear rejection. It is much easier to gripe to someone who is not involved in the situation, portraying ourselves as a victim of what is happening, than to face the possibility of being rejected when we make a request. A Chinese proverb advises, "He who asks is a fool for five minutes, but he who does not ask remains a fool forever." To build bridges in relationships, we need to ask, and to do so directly and only to the person who can resolve the issue.

It must be done in a way that clearly expresses the outcome we seek and, again, it must be done without accusatory energy.

"Would you mind not texting during the movie?" asks for what you want. "How about turning off the gosh-darned cell phone?" is not asking, it's complaining. It is negative energy directed at the other person and it makes him or her less likely to respond favorably. You have invaded that person's world with your words and he or she will be far more likely to counterattack or, minimally, not to comply.

We need to take responsibility for our relationships and hold ourselves accountable for establishing their tone. When we take responsibility for our relationships, we accept that we create them. We are not victims; we are cocreators. Asking creates the potential for the outcome we seek; complaining legitimizes our feeling like a victim and perpetuates the issue.

When we seek to get our needs met, it is vital that we stay with it until we get what we seek. Giving a halfhearted try and then saying, "See, I told you this wouldn't work" validates and perpetuates victimhood. Complaining to others gets them to agree with our plight and legitimizes a lack of action.

Speaking directly and only to the person who can resolve the issue at hand, you take the quickest route to a resolution without the negativity of complaining. When seeking a solution to the issue with the Denver hotel, I spoke to the front desk clerk. However, years ago I probably would have handled this situation quite differently. As funny as it seems now, I most likely would have called my wife to complain. "Can you hear that racket?" I would have shouted, making sure I stood in the part of the room where the sound was loudest. "This is supposed to be one of the finest hotels in Denver and yet there is this earsplitting racket just outside my window. This is unacceptable! Whoever rated this hotel doesn't know what the heck

> Speak directly and only to the person who can resolve the issue.

they're doing!" And I probably would have stayed in that room, miserable and unable to sleep, just to prove how flawed the hotel was. I then would have complained to everyone I spoke to for the next several days about how I had been mistreated. Poor me. Poor victimized me.

You probably know people like this. Okay, honesty time—take a moment and ask yourself, "Am *I* a person like this?" If you are truthful, chances are you will find at least some areas of your life where you have experienced dissatisfaction but, rather than speaking to the person most likely to resolve the issue, you have complained to others.

There are people who have problems with their intimate partner and yet complain about their dissatisfaction to their friends. Others have challenges with their boss but complain to their spouse. Why is this? When we have a problem with someone, why do we complain to someone else? Because we fear being attacked or rejected. We create scenarios in our minds—which is where all relationships exist—wherein our intimate partner responds negatively to the request to meet our needs, verbally chastises us, or maybe even leaves the relationship; or our boss not only says no but holds the request against us in future performance appraisals or possibly even fires us. These frightening scenarios play repeatedly in our minds, preventing us from acting—which in turn ensures that the problem will not be resolved.

As unhappy as we are in the present situation, often we would rather stay where we are than risk rejection or retribution. We are a baby sitting in a soiled diaper and crying to everyone except the person who can offer the change we seek.

Having little if any awareness of what our needs are, the other person continues his or her present course and we remain unfulfilled. We consider speaking up but then play out the possible negative ramifications of doing so and choose to remain quiet except when complaining to a third party. In doing this, we may think

we are talking the issue out when in actuality we are seeking jus-
tification for our position that the other person is wrong.

"You're right," our friends agree, "she sure is moody. How in
the world do you ever put up with her?" Or a spouse might say,
"You're absolutely right. Your boss is a pain in
the neck!" The response we get justifies our dissatisfaction but does not improve things. With
each experience of the situation and the agreement of our friends and family our internal dissatisfaction grows. This pent-up negative energy
combines with the energy of fearful scenarios,
and when we're unable to take the situation any longer, we explode
in a rage. Feeling attacked, the other person counterattacks and
responds exactly as we feared.

> Feeling attacked,
> the other person
> counterattacks and
> responds exactly
> as feared.

The issue could have been resolved simply with little or no an-
guish or pain by informing the other person as to what we desire.
Living Complaint Free and having Complaint Free relationships
does not mean you simply take whatever is presented to you, however unappealing it is. You deserve to have your needs met. But
when you complain, you are telling the other person what you
don't want. And it is nearly impossible for the mind to focus on the
reverse of an idea. The mind does not deal in opposites. Therefore, change "Don't do this" to "Please do that." You'll find it gets
you what you are seeking more readily and with less stress for both
of you.

If you are going to present people with needs you wish to have
fulfilled, you must be willing to hear the requests of others. You
must open yourself up to listening to others when they are dissatisfied. Other people may not be as astute at communication as you
are. They may not know to say "You might not be aware . . ." or
neutral, declarative words to that effect. They may have been afraid
of your response and built up a head of steam before coming to
you. They may cry out like a wet, hungry, or tired baby.

You would not get angry with a baby for crying, so give this person the same compassion. Listen for the need behind the upset.

If the person continues to rant, consider saying, "I get that this is upsetting for you. What is it that you need?" If the person launches into more complaints, repeat as needed: "I get that this is upsetting for you. What is it you need?" Be open; listen. Resist the temptation to hang negative pictures of this person in your relationship.

> "I get that this is upsetting for you. What is it that you need?"

By being willing to hear the needs of others, you will make it more likely that your own needs will be met. There is a spiritual law of giving and receiving. As it says in Matthew 4:24, "The measure with which you give is the measure you will receive." This law does not mean you will necessarily receive back equal measure from this one person to whom you have been tolerant and compassionate, but the Universe will balance in your favor. You will begin to notice that others are more receptive to hearing from you and providing what you seek.

Jerry Zvacek lives this. Jerry and his wife, Pat, live a few houses down from the first home we purchased in Holden, Missouri, and even before we unpacked, Jerry came by to introduce himself and offer any assistance we might need. Jerry's offer was not perfunctory "welcome to the neighborhood" hospitality. When Jerry says, "If there is anything you need, let me know," he means it.

The home we purchased was over a hundred years old and in constant need of repair. One day we noticed a leak in the roof of our front porch. Whenever it rained, water streamed through the roof and soaked our porch swing and chairs and left puddles on the floor. We became concerned that the floor might rot through. Once when Jerry stopped by to "check up on us"—his words for seeing if we needed anything—I mentioned the leak.

"My son, Mike, is a roofer by trade," Jerry said. "I can call and get him to fix it." I had heard roof repair was expensive and didn't want to admit that I was unsure if I had enough money at that time to pay a professional, so I demurred, saying I would do it myself. The only problem was that I had no idea how to repair a leaky roof. I purchased a skid of shingles from a home repair store, asked a clerk there for basic information on reshingling, and set to work.

I did my best to tear off the old roof and staple down a new tarpaper base. About the time I was ready to begin applying shingles I noticed Jerry at the base of the ladder smiling up at me.

"How's it going?" he asked.

"Fine," I lied. I really had no idea how to begin to put the shingles on the roof or overlap them properly to ensure a watertight result.

"You know how to cut those and stick 'em down, right?" he asked.

"Um . . . no," I admitted.

Jerry climbed the ladder, grabbed my razor knife, and showed me how to cut and tack down the shingles. I followed his advice while he stood at the top of the ladder encouraging and guiding me through the process. A short time later, I noticed Jerry's son pull up in front of our house. Jerry yelled a greeting down to Mike and they began to talk as I continued working on the roof.

I'm not certain exactly how or when it happened, but in a very short time Jerry and Mike were no longer on the ground watching me work; they were beside me applying the shingles at a blinding pace. Soon after that I found myself on the ground watching as they finished the job. Without waiting to be thanked or for me to offer payment, Jerry and Mike gathered up their tools, smiled, and said "See you later."

That's Jerry. He is always looking for what others need and asking himself how he might help. In doing this, Jerry finds a great deal of satisfaction and inner peace. Most dissatisfaction comes from being wrapped up in ourselves. Jerry is wrapped up in others and, as a result, leads a simple and contented life.

One hot summer day I was out mowing our lawn. I was in the middle of cutting a large, ever-narrowing circle, keeping the wheels of my lawn tractor inside the shorn groove left by my previous pass. At one point, I noticed that my previous swath seemed to be twice as large as I would have expected. I decided I must have been lost in thought and not realized how much grass I had cut. I took another trip around the yard only to find again that the area of cut grass was larger than I expected. Several more times I went around the circle and noticed that with each pass the grass seemed to be getting mowed twice as fast as I would have expected.

> Most dissatisfaction comes from being too wrapped up in ourselves.

As I was nearly finished, I caught a glimpse of something out of the corner of my eye and spun around to see Jerry following behind me on his own lawn tractor. Jerry and his son-in-law, Joel, share a riding mower and Jerry had been driving the mower past our house to deliver it to Joel when he saw me cutting my grass. I was mowing my lawn and Jerry was on a mower. This was too great an opportunity for Jerry to let pass. He fell in behind me on his mower, cutting my grass right behind me. Over the noise, I had no idea he was doing this and I'm sure to passing cars we must have looked like synchronized yard contractors. We took turns cutting the last rectangle of grass and then Jerry smiled, tipped his hat, and without a word drove back out onto the street in the direction of Joel's house.

Jerry thinks of others first. He does not dwell on his unmet needs. Instead, he is grateful for what he has and his focus is on what he can do to help others. Jerry is probably the happiest person I have ever met and his relaxed nature comes from his focus being on those around him rather than on himself.

Early on the morning of Saturday, February 21, 2004, Jerry was out cutting down trees on his property in Holden, Missouri. He cut through the base of a tall tree and watched it begin to fall, but it got caught in the branches of an adjacent tree. Jerry planned to cut down the supporting tree next, so he revved up his chain saw and went back to work. The vibrations of the saw against the base of the supporting tree dislodged the first tree, which came thundering down on Jerry crushing him.

Jerry couldn't move. He knew he was badly hurt. Blood poured from his broken nose and coated his glasses. He struggled to stand but could not. He was trapped beneath a thousand pounds of timber. Jerry shouted for someone to rescue him but he was too far out; no one could hear his cries. He drifted in and out of consciousness, causing him to lose track of time. After a few hours, he shoved a small stick into the ground to serve as a sundial. He watched his makeshift timekeeper as its shadow moved slowly along the ground until there was no more daylight to cast a shadow.

As the sun set, the temperature began to drop and Jerry lay under that tree with nothing to keep him company except his pain and his thoughts. Years before, another man in Holden had been similarly crushed by a tree and was now a quadriplegic. "Is that how I'm going to end up?" Jerry wondered.

At seven o'clock that evening Jerry's wife, Pat, noticed his truck was home but Jerry was not. It was not like Jerry to be late for a meal; Pat wondered if he might be off working late somewhere on their 90 acres. "But why after dark?" she wondered. Their son-in-law, Joel, stopped by and Pat asked if he had seen Jerry.

"No," replied Joel, "but I'll go look for him." He grabbed a flashlight and walked out into the cold evening to search for Jerry.

"Jerry!" cried Joel, slicing through the darkness with the beam from his flashlight. "Hello . . . Jerry!"

Inside Pat sat at the kitchen table, arms crossed, wondering, "Now, where is that man?" It was a shame that Joel would be late for his own supper because he was out searching for Jerry, who had probably just lost track of time. "But that isn't like Jerry," she thought.

Meanwhile, Joel was outside looking. "Jerry!" he shouted. Silence.

Walking faster to cover more ground and to help stave off the cold, Joel began to wonder, "Maybe a friend picked him up and they're down at the Harmony House smoking cigarettes and swapping tall tales." But that was not like Jerry. Yes, he loved to sit at the small restaurant and chase his cigarettes with coffee while sharing whoppers with the other men of the town. But it wasn't like him not to tell Pat where he was going.

For the first time, Joel began to worry. "Jerry!" he said in a voice that was more like a prayer than a shout. Then he heard a low guttural sound. Was it one of the cows? He stood stock still and shouted at the top of his lungs, "Jerry!" He heard the sound again. It wasn't a cow. It was a voice.

"I'm over here," Jerry said weakly.

Joel ran toward the voice but the illumination from his flashlight showed only a twisted mass of branches. "Jerry?"

"I'm here," said Jerry as Joel trained the beam on him and the tree under which he had lain for more than seven hours.

Joel rushed back to the house to call for paramedics. When she heard what had happened, Pat grabbed another flashlight and rushed out into the night to be with her husband.

Jerry had a crushed leg and both shoulders were broken. His collar bone was shattered. Three of his vertebrae were crushed and he had five broken ribs. He had been in excruciating pain, with nothing to eat or drink, for hours.

Jerry had every reason to yell, curse, and complain. But when Pat arrived, Jerry's first words to her were *not* "Look what happened to me!" He did *not* say, "Thank God you've come!" He *didn't* say, "Help me, I think I'm dying." Nor did Jerry say, "It's about damned time!"

No. The first thing Jerry said to Pat, without a trace of sarcasm, was simply, "So, dear, how was your day?" And he meant it. Jerry is just hardwired that way. His first thought was of Pat's well-being and not himself. He sincerely wanted to know how her day had been.

The recovery process was long and arduous. Jerry was bedridden for over a month. In time he was able to amble around first with a walker, then with two canes, and finally with one cane. Once he was again able to drive, he began to stop by our house to "check up on us." During all that time, I never once heard Jerry complain about his ordeal. I brought this up to him one afternoon and he said, "Oh, there were a couple of days right after it happened that I threw myself a great big pity party. But it didn't help, so I quit showing up for those parties."

Steadying himself on his canes, Jerry smiled and said, "Will, there's enough griping in the world without me adding to it. And this world has given me a lot of gifts. I think one of the greatest gifts I can give back to this ol' world is not to add to all the whining and bitching that goes on."

You said it, Jerry.

Opening Up

1. For the next 24 hours, note how often you convey your needs to others by expressing dissatisfaction over the way things are rather than asking for what you want.

2. Make a list of what you desire. Then consider ways you might ask for what you want that focus on the ideal outcome rather than the current situation. For example, if you want help cleaning the house, instead of saying,

"You never do anything around here—this house would be a pigsty if it weren't for me," consider saying, "I need some help. Would you be responsible for vacuuming the house once a week and doing three loads of laundry?"

3. When faced with something that bothers you, say, "You're probably not aware of this . . . ," and express your observation in a neutral fashion.

4. Be willing to face rejection by asking for what you want. You'll be amazed at how readily people comply when asked nicely. Try "I need . . ." and "Would you please . . . ?"

5. Remember Jerry. Every day for the next week, put someone else's needs ahead of your own. Rather than insisting others watch your favorite TV show, watch theirs. Do this without drawing attention to yourself and without any expectation of reciprocity. Journal about how this makes you feel and what positive results you find for yourself and your relationships.

CHAPTER 4

Why We G.R.I.P.E.

*I do not want people to be agreeable, as it saves
me the trouble of liking them.*

—Jane Austen

You deserve healthy, open, mutually satisfying relationships; relationships that support your dreams and celebrate your unique and individual path; relationships that are honest and void of taxing personal agendas; relationships that nurture your spirit and replenish your soul.

Complaining has no place in such ideal relationships.

As previously discussed, complaining perpetuates negative behavior and creates discord and dissatisfaction. And according to an article in the April 2009 issue of *Men's Health* magazine, people who are in an intimate relationship where there is a lot of complaining are more likely to cheat on their partner. Quoting Dr. Elizabeth Allen, of the University of Colorado, who studied communication between partners about to get married, one indicator of their future fidelity was the ratio of positive to negative interactions with each other.

Complaining is corrosive to the bonds that unite people. Yet for many, complaining is woven into the fabric of their connections. People waste much of their precious time complaining to and about one another as well as griping about life in general. This griping is not only damaging to the relationship but also damaging to those within the relationship. A recent study at the University of Missouri found that teenage girls whose relationships were based primarily on complaining (about their parents, teachers, peers, etc.) tended to suffer significantly higher rates of depression.

In "Complaints and Complaining: Functions, Antecedents, and Consequences," which appeared in *Psychological Bulletin* in 1996, Dr. Robin Kowalski wrote, "Many complaints do not reflect people's true attitudes toward the object or person but rather involve attempts to elicit particular interpersonal reactions." These "interpersonal reactions" are easily remembered by the acronym G.R.I.P.E.:

Get Attention

Remove responsibility

Inspire envy

Power

Excuse poor performance

When you hear yourself or someone else complain, try to determine what the underlying motivation might be. Ask yourself, "What interpersonal reaction is this complaint attempting to elicit? What do they need or want?" You will find that complaining is often a misplaced attempt to get a social or psychological need met. Ask yourself, "Under which of the five categories does that complaint fall?" We are complex psychological beings, and you will find that a complaint may fit in several of these categories at the same time.

<u>G</u>et Attention

"Hey, notice me!" should be tattooed on everyone's forehead. Getting attention from others is a desire we all possess. We all need to connect with others and receiving attention affirms that connection. Mary Kay Ash, founder of Mary Kay cosmetics, said, "There are two things people want more than sex and money—recognition and praise."

I was delivering a speech to representatives of the Canadian government and was scheduled to do a book signing after my speech. Because it was such a large group, rather than my sponsors handling the book sales, they brought in a bookstore that was part of a major Canadian chain. While waiting to be introduced, I struck up a conversation with Pierre, the manager of the bookstore.

"How's your store doing?" I asked.

"Great!" Pierre said. "Our store consistently outperforms all of the other stores in our chain by as much as three to one based on sales per square foot."

"You must be in a great location," I said.

"No, we're actually in a poor location," he said. "It's kind of hard to find our store."

"Then are you in an affluent section of town?" I asked.

"No, we're in an area of town that's about average economically."

I was confused. "Then how do you manage to sell so many books compared to other stores in your chain?"

"I think it's because of the way we treat our customers," Pierre said. "Every time a customer is within three meters [about ten feet] of one of our employees, the

> Yeah. I called her up. She gave me a bunch of crap about me not listening to her or something. I don't know— I wasn't really paying attention.
>
> —COMEDIAN HARRY DUNN

employee is expected to greet them. Nothing special—just 'Hi,' 'How's it going?' etc."

"That's it?" I asked.

"Yeah," he said. "It's not uncommon for someone who's in our store for twenty minutes to be greeted sixteen times."

"Sixteen times?" I said incredulously. "With all that attention, doesn't it make them feel like you're trying to sell them something?"

Pierre's smile was friendly and sincere, although his eyes expressed how naive he thought I was. "Mr. Bowen," he said, "we *are* trying to sell them something. We're a bookstore. And they came into our store to buy something. We're just making it a pleasant experience by giving them what everyone craves."

"Which is . . . ?" I asked.

"Attention," Pierre said. "People want to be recognized. Nothing tells a person they matter as much as simply acknowledging their presence. At my store, we do this by saying hello. We don't try to push books on them. We just let them know that we notice them by saying hi again and again. As a result, they feel important and they buy lots of books from us."

You've heard it said that there's safety in numbers. Human beings are herd animals. We need to feel like we belong, and being acknowledged by others tells us that we do. This is why it is sometimes difficult to leave an unhealthy relationship. Being with someone, however painful the situation may be, makes us feel we belong; we have a place. And, we reason, it's better than being alone.

Something in our DNA tells us that we need to be connected and associated with other people. We feel we are safe when we are with others; we are okay. And how do we know we've been accepted by others? We receive acknowledgment. We get attention.

As we've discussed, relationships with other people are not a want but a need. This is why we feel uncomfortable when we step into an elevator with someone we don't know. We are in close proximity with someone but the relationship has not been formalized. We have not acknowledged the other person, nor has he or she acknowledged us. We feel the connection with the other person in the elevator needs to be made, and so most people will do whatever they can think of to build a bridge. Typically, they will complain. They will make a negative remark about the weather ("Man, is it ever going to stop raining?") or about the local sports franchise ("Boy, the Giants sure stunk up the place last night") in an attempt to acknowledge the other person and elicit a response. The conversation needn't go further and rarely does. The tension has been broken because the connection has been made. Both parties have been acknowledged.

Many people who have taken the challenge to become Complaint Free have found that being with friends and family members presents a challenge because they are so accustomed to getting attention by opening conversations with negative statements. They complain about what happened at work, they complain about their children's behavior, they complain about their health, the weather, politics, other drivers . . . the list is endless. This is a default mode employed to get attention from the other person. Regardless of what they are saying, the real message is "Hey, notice me!"

Best-selling author Joe Vitale told me that after becoming aware of the proclivity of people to connect through complaining, he developed a simple new strategy for breaking the ice. "I compliment them," he said. "It doesn't have to be a big thing. I was once on an elevator and it was raining outside. The man standing next to me had a nice umbrella and I told him I liked it. The man smiled and for the remainder of the ride we discussed umbrellas—it was nice. And rather than stir up negative energies by complaining, we both felt a little happier for having met one another." The "elevator ice" was broken with warmth rather than the energy-draining negativity of a complaint.

You can't go wrong with a compliment. If the other person is someone you barely know or someone with whom you have a professional relationship, it is best that the compliments be about a material object (the person's shoes, briefcase, cell phone, etc.) rather than a physical attribute. Most people are very uncomfortable with a compliment about their bodies or anything of a personal nature. Comments such as "What beautiful earrings" or "Those are great shoes. Where did you get them?" tend to be perceived as nonthreatening. But make sure your energy really is nonthreatening. Be certain you're not subtly hitting on the other person unless you're prepared to deal with the consequences.

A compliment about someone's behavior is always welcome. "You always smile so warmly; you just light up the room" not only gives the person attention but reinforces a behavior and makes him or her more likely to repeat it. "You are always on time. That's one of the many things I appreciate about you" is another example. A compliment must be sincere. Otherwise, you'll be written off as manipulative or sarcastic.

Of course, when it comes to people with whom you share a more intimate relationship, you can and should be freer with your compliments. Even if your intimate partner is wearing an outfit you've seen dozens of times, if you like the way he or she looks in it, say so. This will build a connection that reinforces the relationship and your partner's positive feelings toward you.

My family and I live in Kearney, Missouri, a small town on the outskirts of Kansas City. Kearney is famous for the historic outlaw Jesse James being buried across the street from our grocery store. One of the things we enjoy about living in a small town is that most people wave at you as you drive past them. Typically, it's someone you have not met and never will meet, yet that wave says, "You're acknowledged; I notice you." When this happens, the recipient internalizes the gesture, however perfunctory it may be, as, "I'm okay. I belong. I'm safe."

What does it mean to get attention from someone? It typically means to get that person to look at you, perhaps speak to you, to somehow engage with you as a human being. In the many workshops and conversations I have been to I find a consensus that trying to get attention is the primary reason people gripe. Therefore, I have a warning to convey. In our current technological society, attention (or, as it's called in the cyberworld, "face time") is becoming more endangered than the Brazilian rain forest. Look around and you'll see people staring at the screens of their smart phones rather than giving even a passing glance to those they are with.

Just for fun, the next time you are in a public place, count the number of people who are looking at their BlackBerry, iPhone, or other device. (Maybe it'd be faster to count those who *aren't*.) In restaurants, parks, movie theaters, bowling alleys, and sports arenas they sit in a trancelike stupor checking sports scores, sending email, answering texts, playing games, or surfing the Web. Rather than talk with their date, friends, or family with whom they have chosen to spend time, they are texting someone who is not even there. As you drive, notice how often you see multiple people sitting in the same car but each talking on cell phones to people who are not present.

Beyond the safety issues of not watching the road while driving, the misuse of gadgets is robbing us of a basic human need: attention. Over the last generation, connecting as a family at the dinner table has diminished as people eat at drive-throughs or sit in front of the television while eating meals, their attention on the television rather than one another. The results of this trend are alarming. The benefits of eating a meal together sans technology are rapidly dissolving.

This time of connecting while eating has many benefits. According to a survey conducted by researchers at the University of Minnesota that appeared in the August 2004 issue of the *Archives of Pediatrics and Adolescent Medicine,* frequent family meals are related to better nutritional intake and a decreased risk of unhealthy weight control practices and substance abuse.

Marla Eisenberg of Project EAT (Eating Among Teens), a research project for the American Psychological Association that studied eating habits of teenagers, found that the frequency with which a teenager eats meals with his or her family appears to be associated with a variety of psychosocial and behavioral benefits. Teens who eat with their families are much less likely to engage in cigarette smoking or alcohol and marijuana abuse. They tend to have better grades in school, fewer depressive symptoms, less suicidal ideation, and fewer suicide attempts. Eating together without the distraction of television allows parents to model healthy eating, which nourishes the teenager's body, but more important, the teen gets the attention that feeds their souls.

"What went well for you today?"

When we realized that complaining about the day's events was the default opening conversational salvo at our own dinner table, my family began a new dinner ritual. We now look at one another and ask, in turn, "What went well for you today?" That gets the conversation going in a tone that leaves us feeling energized rather than depleted by complaining during our time together.

Regardless of the depth or brevity of the connection, people with whom you have relationships need attention from you. And as you give them the attention they crave, they may complain less and you will find that you will begin to receive the attention you need as well.

Remove Responsibility

During the 1970s, many television shows cultivated a catchphrase that viewers would wait intently to hear each week. A TV star saying, "God will get you for this, Walter," "Dy-no-mite!" or "You bet your sweet bippy" would send both the studio and home audiences into peals of laughter. Actor/comedian Freddie Prinze starred in a popular show which aired from 1974 to 1977 titled *Chico and the Man.* Embellishing his Puerto Rican accent, Prinze, who played a car mechanic, would utter his famous phrase whenever faced with doing something he didn't want to do. "It's not my job!" he would say as the studio audience laughed and applauded enthusiastically.

Complaining is often done to absolve a person of responsibility. Complaints express, "It's not my job. I'm not culpable. I'm not responsible."

Children in the United States used to play a popular game called hot potato. One child would grab a ball, shout, "Hot potato!" and pass the ball quickly to another child. The kid who caught the ball would shout, "Hot potato!" and toss it as fast as possible to someone else. Around and around, the "potato" was thrown and caught. It was imagined to be so "hot" that whoever caught it would burn their hands if they did not toss it away quickly. If a child dropped the "potato," she or he was out of the game.

People complain as a way of playing societal and relationship hot potato. They think that their negative statement about an issue at hand removes them from the responsibility of seeking a positive resolution. Their complaint says, "It's not my job. I'm passing it on to you!" They complain to someone and feel their responsibility has been fulfilled. They are the canary in the coal mine. Having pointed out the problem, their task is complete; the resolution of the issue belongs to the person to whom they have complained.

This might be effective if it resulted in the person receiving the complaint solving the problem. But that person, too, will typically play hot potato with the issue, passing it off to someone else. Each person having pointed out the challenge feels they have accomplished something but all they have done is to remove themselves from being liable; they have taken themselves out of the picture when it comes to creating a resolution.

In our church, people used to come to me frequently to complain about any of a variety of things. I soon began to say, "I'm glad you noticed this issue. What are you going to do to make it better?" Their deer-in-the-headlights look conveyed great meaning: "*Do* something? I just did something—I told you. This hot potato is all yours!" I soon found that asking what the complainers planned to do to make things better cut down on a lot of complaining. I reminded them that they were able to improve anything they found distasteful.

You probably know people who have complained to you about some problem in their life. You may have found that if you make a suggestion about something they might try, they immediately complain about your suggestion, telling you how your idea will not work. Genuinely wanting to help them, you then make another recommendation, which they again shoot down, complaining about the impracticality of your idea. After several attempts to advise people like this, you realize that they really don't want to improve the situation; they want you to bear witness to their belief that the situation is unresolvable. There is nothing they can do. Therefore, they are off the hook. They are victims and are putting you and the world on notice that they are not and could not be responsible for fixing the problem.

> My philosophy is that not only are you responsible for your life, but doing the best at this moment puts you in the best place for the next moment.
>
> —OPRAH WINFREY

Author and visionary Michael Beckwith has said that the lowest level of spiritual growth is victimhood. People see themselves as victims of others or the world around them, and of circumstances. Complaining is used to perpetuate this belief and it keeps them from attempting to make things better. This is why people so often complain about those they are in a relationship with. By complaining about coworkers, family, spouse, and friends people are saying, "That's the way they are. And nothing I do can change them." If you make helpful recommendations, their complaints become more strident in an attempt to prove their lack of control and relieve them of the responsibility of making any attempt to improve the relationship.

> Complaining lets a brute know that a victim is in the neighborhood.
>
> —DR. MAYA ANGELOU

Think of someone you complain about frequently. Is the thing that bugs you about this person universally true about him or her? Does the person behave this way with everyone? If he or she is different with someone else, what is different about his or her relationship with this other person and how can you cultivate such a relationship? How might you soften your approach if necessary? Or how might you stand strong in your convictions and clearly express your needs without blaming or shaming the other person? What can you do to draw out of the other person the respect and treatment you deserve?

Relationships are not a 50/50 proposition. They are 100/100. You are 100 percent responsible for your relationships. The best definition I've ever heard for *responsible* is "able to respond." In any relationship, you are able to respond—there is something you can do to improve it. Complaining negates your ability to respond by excusing you from trying. Your response may not work the first time. It may not work every time. But through your efforts you discover ways of guiding the relationship that work for you. Best-selling author Wayne Dyer said, "You get treated in life the way you teach people to treat you." Accept that you are teaching people to treat you as they are treating you and begin to ask yourself what you can change to shift the experience. What are you not giving the other person so he or she will respond in a way that meets your needs? How are you able to respond?

When I was a young child one of my favorite Sunday school stories was David and Goliath. Being a small boy myself, I was inspired by the tale of how a kid like me had managed to defeat a giant of a man with only a sling and a stone. I was told this was because God favored David and therefore David prevailed.

Much later in life I reread the story and discovered a much deeper and more profound meaning. According to 1 Samuel, Goliath offered to fight any Israelite soldier who dared face him. The winner of this two-man skirmish would decide the outcome of the war; there needn't be a protracted fight with thousands killed on both sides. But, feeling they were incapable of defeating the giant Philistine, not one Israelite took up the challenge, and so the battle raged on. Goliath stomped back and forth along the battle lines urging someone, *anyone,* to fight him but the Israelite soldiers ran past him to fight the other Philistines instead.

> Relationships are not 50/50. They are 100/100.

Then along came young David, a shepherd boy. When David first told his brothers of his intent to fight Goliath, they warned him he could not defeat the giant. David's brothers had not themselves tried to fight Goliath but they knew it was impossible.

QUESTION: Have you ever had a friend or family member tell you it's impossible to improve a relationship?

David then approached King Saul, who similarly said that Goliath could not be defeated. Nonetheless, Saul told David that if he was going to try, he should wear Saul's armor.

QUESTION: Have you ever had others who themselves do not have happy, successful relationships but insist on telling you how to improve yours?

David ignored his brothers' advice and dropped Saul's armor. The boy approached the giant and secured victory with only a stone and a sling.

What came to me as I read this story as an adult was that David was probably not the only one who could have defeated Goliath. *But he was the only one who tried!*

God (or Spirit, the Universe, or whatever you choose to call it) did not play favorites with David then and does not play favorites now. You *are* able to respond. Don't listen to those who say that you cannot do things to improve your relationships. Don't listen to people who have failed repeatedly themselves but seem intent on advising you on how to have successful relationships. I have a friend who was divorced four times by age forty, yet he consistently wanted to give me marital advice. I finally silenced his unsolicited suggestions by telling him, "Look, you're trying to tell me how to rodeo and you've been bucked off every horse you've ever ridden."

His response was classic: "It wasn't me—it was the women I married." He then complained for an hour and half about the many flaws of each of the women he had the misfortune to have wed. I tried to point out that he chose the women he married but he had complaints as to why this was not entirely true. He had given up all responsibility for his marriages and so will probably repeat the same issue in future relationships. Last I heard he was on wife number five.

Oft-quoted spiritual author William Arthur Ward wrote,

> *The pessimist complains about the wind;*
> *The optimist expects it to change;*
> *And the realist adjusts the sails.*

You have the power in any relationship to adjust your sails by taking responsibility for the course of the relationship.

Inspire Envy

Behind many a complaint is a thinly disguised crow of superiority. The complainer implies, "There is something wrong with you because you are not like me." Many complaints are a subtle, negative comparison between someone else and the person doing the griping. The complainer is covertly stating, "I don't have the flaw about which I'm complaining; don't you wish you were like me?"

COMPLAINT:	"My new boss is incompetent."
TRANSLATION:	"I'm far more capable that she is."
COMPLAINT:	"You always take so long to get ready."
TRANSLATION:	"I'm organized and punctual."
COMPLAINT:	"Those idiots at the water department have messed up our bill again."
TRANSLATION:	"If I worked there, things would be done right."
COMPLAINT:	"You're so stupid."
TRANSLATION:	"I'm so smart."

People complain to inspire envy. As such, complaining is bragging. You may be talking negatively about another person but you are really saying that you are better than him or her and you want others to notice and appreciate your superiority.

People gripe about others and situations to brag. If you question this, think about the drivers who upset you in traffic. You don't complain about people who drive like you. Rather, you complain about people who *don't* drive like you. If you tend to drive fast and assertively, slow and cautious drivers can have you yelling through the windshield. If you tend to drive more slowly, drivers zipping by you may inspire you to mutter expletives under your breath.

My wife, Gail, and I have very different styles when it comes to driving. I tend to drive fast and Gail drives in a way I consider to be painfully slow. I drive just slow enough to avoid getting a speeding ticket, whereas my perspective is that Gail drives just fast enough to avoid getting a parking ticket. When she is driving me to the airport I find myself staring out the window and thinking, "Would you please speed up? For goodness' sake, gum wrappers are passing us!" When I drive, I can tell Gail is equally bothered, as evidenced by the fingernail claw marks in the dashboard and the look of sheer terror on her face.

A cry of superiority is, in reality, often a whimper of insecurity. Complaining to brag is a way of saying, "Please tell me I'm okay because right now, or in this area of my life, I don't feel that I am." If you notice that a person is complaining to brag, listen for the attribute he or she is criticizing. Make a mental note that this person is probably not feeling rock solid in this way him- or herself. For example, if your friend makes a catty remark about the way someone dresses, consider that your friend might not feel attractively dressed, and try complimenting your friend's clothes. If coworkers complain about a task they feel was performed unsatisfactorily, consider how they might be feeling they are not performing at their peak, and try to find a way to give them genuine positive feedback in this area.

When people confront you and begin to complain, consider that they may be attempting to make themselves look better. Don't get dragged into an argument. Have you ever considered that an argument is nothing more than negative energetic statements (complaints) hurled back and forth? Don't take the bait. Take a deep breath and let their negative energy pass by. You don't have to show up for every fight you are invited to. Their criticism is an attempt to inflate their negative self-image.

When a person belittles you or something you have done with a complaint, remember that this may be disguised bragging, which in turn means the person is not feeling good about him- or herself. By itself, that realization can negate the destructive effect those complaining words have on you. When you see a person attempting to boost his or her deflated ego, you react very differently than if you see a person who has inside knowledge about some negative aspect of you.

> You don't have to show up for every fight you are invited to.

In our society, most levels of accomplishment and competency are measured compared to something or someone else. A person who complains to brag is saying, "Compared to that other person, I'm better." If someone is directing these complaints at you, you have a choice. You can counter with a complaint or criticism of your own, which will further weaken the relationship, or you can realize that the person has launched this missile because he or she already feels inferior. Letting it pass allows you to win without fighting, which, according to ancient Chinese war tactician Sun Tzu, is "the best of skills."

When you catch yourself complaining, do some reflecting to see if you are complaining to elevate yourself. Are you trying to prove that you are superior? Are you implying that you are smarter, more organized, friendlier, better dressed, more punctual? If so, this is a call to improve in the areas you feel lacking. Your attempt to prove your superiority is a testament to your feeling of inferiority in the area you are complaining about.

Our complaining can allow us to discover needs we have not yet sought to have fulfilled. Our complaints, therefore, can be a productive signal for us *if* we are willing to catch them and do a little digging within ourselves to discover their cause. Ideally, of course, we should investigate our feelings and discover such things without the "ear pollution" we create when we complain.

In a letter to one of his friends, Mark Twain wrote, "Thunder is good, thunder is impressive; but it is lightning that does the work." Complaint bragging is thunder. It's loud and gets your attention but it is hollow and without substance.

But from the sound of the thunder, we can discover the course of the lightning and harness its power.

> To win without fighting is the best of skills.
>
> —SUN TZU

Power

Complaining is a very effective way to garner power.

Few in history have accrued and galvanized power more effectively or with more tragic results than Adolf Hitler.

QUESTION: How was an Austrian-born former sign painter able to amass supreme authority over Germany and incite war against much of the world?

ANSWER: By complaining.

In *Mein Kampf,* Hitler wrote,

> The art of leadership, as displayed by really great popular leaders in all ages, consists in consolidating the attention of the people against a single adversary [*complaining*] and taking care that nothing will split up that attention into sections. The more the militant energies of the people are directed towards one objective the more will new recruits join the movement, attracted by the magnetism of its unified action, and thus the striking power will be all the more enhanced.

In his passionate and vitriolic speeches, Hitler sought to create an adversary against which most Germans could rally. He oversimplified Germany's post–World War I problems, placing them on the backs of the "mongrel races." He evoked passionate support for the belief that non-Aryans, especially Jews, were the cause of any and all problems. In his writings and his speeches, Hitler detailed his vision for a racially pure world dominated by Aryan people. He convinced his audiences that the Aryan race was the last hope for the survival of humanity. Again and again he complained and drew most of his nation into believing that the future of their country and the world was at stake. Hitler wielded supreme power with his rhetoric.

In relationships, people use their complaints to win you over to their side, giving them power over others. Someone in your family who is upset with another family member may complain to you about the other person to ensure your support should it ever be needed. The complainer is building a base of power.

People complain to coworkers to get support against management or other employees. If it ever comes down to "them or me," they want to make sure they have solidified your support and given you ample reason to make it "them or us."

We see complaining used to gain power here in the United States during election season. Negative, complaining advertising assaults us from every front, attempting to sway our vote. Why is such negativity poured through the airwaves? Because it works. But not necessarily in the way you might think. If you are a diehard supporter of a political party, the other party is not so naive as to believe that their negative ads will shift you to their side. Rather, the negative advertising is designed to disgust you so much with your own party's candidate that you don't vote. Either way, the complaining party still moves one vote closer to the office it seeks. This is not a new phenomenon. In *Nods and Becks,* published in 1944, Franklin P. Adams wrote, "Elections are won by men and women

> Dwelling on the negative simply contributes to its power.
>
> —SHIRLEY MacLAINE

chiefly because most people vote against somebody rather than for somebody."

.   As you look into the reasons for people's complaining, you begin to notice that people, as mentioned earlier, complain to excuse themselves from responsibility. They will give you a litany of reasons why they cannot and should not be held responsible for improving a situation. Then they will ramp up the complaining to entice others to join them in their unwillingness to act. This is complaining to gain power—power against taking action to change a self-imposed limitation. They will attempt to build a base of support for their reluctance to improve a relationship.

Someone will complain about a person and, in so doing, define that person a certain way. The complaint may be that the other person does not listen, tends to run late, is too brusque, is too messy, speaks too fast, speaks too little, jumps to conclusions, whatever. Having defined the person, the complainer has no responsibility to consider how his or her interactions with this person may be causing the very behavior being complained about. In a sense, complainers have vaccinated themselves against a solution.

But somewhere inside they know that they have done this— that they have taken the coward's way out by pointing the finger of complaint at the other person rather than seeking a harmonious relationship. They then feel a need to justify and legitimize this faulty premise and they begin to complain to others in an effort to get them to support this position.

Recently, our church went through a strategic planning process to clarify our purpose and vision and to discern a three-to-five-year course of action. The first thing we did was conduct forty-five-minute interviews with anyone and everyone who wished to share their feelings and dreams for our ministry. We sent out letters to all and announced the interviews in every medium we had at our disposal for several weeks. Then over the next six months we invited everyone to five separate daylong meetings to share and dream our destiny together. We had hundreds of people get involved and the resulting plan was compelling and inspiring.

But there were a handful of people who were very upset about the direction we are taking and they were growing ever more strident in their complaints. When the church leadership first heard of these complaints, we were concerned that perhaps we had not taken into account what these people had to say. We wondered if somehow we had not done an effective job listening to everyone. We found it odd that rather than talking to us, they were complaining to others who, likewise, had chosen not to participate in the interviews or any of the meetings and discussions.

We realized that by complaining during the discernment process, they excused themselves from the responsibility of participating and the responsibility of doing the work that was decided upon. They stood on the sidelines complaining, which excused them from being responsible for the outcome. That much we understood. But why were they complaining even more now that things had been decided and were moving forward? Further, why were they calling other people who had not participated in the process and complaining to them?

We realized they were complaining to legitimize their inactivity. The complainers were attempting to gather power over likeminded people who similarly chose not to get involved. This was meant to assuage their stinging egos, which were telling them that if this was important to them, they should have invested the time to participate. They knew that complaining about the way things were going would not generate enough power to change the course that lay ahead. But they could complain to legitimize their inactivity; they were attempting to have power over their own guilt. They were trying to save face and there is no power more enticing than the power to save face.

Be careful of complaints because they are often used to have power over you or someone else. Solid relationships are based on mutual respect and a feeling of safety. These attributes are not to be found in a power struggle. Robert Frost wrote, "The strongest and most effective force in guaranteeing the long-term mainte-nance of power is not violence in all the forms deployed by the dominant to control the dominated, but consent in all the forms in which the dominated acquiesce in their own domination." In relationships, don't acquiesce to someone else by allowing yourself to be swayed by their complaining. Get the facts; make up your own mind.

Excuse Poor Performance

People will complain to excuse themselves from doing well at something. They may do this in advance of attempting a task or, if they are not currently performing well, they will complain to justify poor results.

Again, to quote Dr. Robin Kowalski of Clemson University, "People may save face by using complaints as self-handicapping strategies. . . . If a student complains of illness the night before a test, he or she has set up an excuse in the event of poor perform-ance on the test."

Have you ever spoken to someone in the morning and asked, "How are you?" Immediately you begin to regret having asked be-cause from the look on the other person's face you can tell he or she is about to unload on you.

"I'll tell you how I'm doing. My neighbor's dog kept me up *all night* with its barking. As a result, I overslept. I then put on my new blue shirt and while I was in the bathroom I got toothpaste down the front of it!" Their voice rising in tone and energy they continue, "So I went to put on my white shirt but it was wrinkled. I tried to iron it and burned two fingers!" Holding up their singed digits, they continue their rant barely stopping to breathe between sentences. "I then went out into the garage only to discover that my daughter had left the car's headlights on, so the damn battery was dead. I managed to get a jump for the battery and then while driving in to work another car cut me off and I spilled coffee down the front of my newly ironed white shirt. Then I . . ."

On and on it continues. You catch yourself thinking, "Maybe if I fake a heart attack, they'll stop complaining to me."

Is this person really trying to update you on his or her status? No. What this person is doing is putting you on notice. The implied message behind this frenetic diatribe is "Don't expect me to be pleasant or productive for the rest of this day." This person has ensured a day void of positive connections or industrious results and the day's work hasn't even begun yet.

People will complain about their work environment as a means of distracting management from their poor performance. By repeatedly making negative comments about the conditions under which they are forced to work, they are able to get away with substandard production. I received the following email from Alden Clark, owner of the Salon on Kirby in Houston, Texas. He had heard me speak and then took the 21-day Complaint Free program back to his staff.

> I can pretty much guarantee that almost every salon across this planet is known for its employee break room, "the den of inequity." It is the spot where employees gather to complain, complain, and complain.
>
> On New Year's Eve 2007, I went up to the salon, painted the break room purple, and stenciled "A Complaint Free World" on the wall. As each employee arrived on January 2 I gave them a CD of your speech, a copy of your book, and a Complaint Free bracelet. I told them to listen and to read what they could, and I showed them

the chart I made with everyone's name on it and counting the twenty-one days. I then let them know there would be a reward for everyone who finished the twenty-one days.

The first week was fun for everyone. The second week I panicked! By Wednesday three people quit, saying, "If you are not going to confront the problems in the salon, then we don't want to work here anymore." I held the door open as I escorted them out. I spent some time in prayer and meditation that night, making sure I was doing the right thing. The three that quit were my three biggest complainers. The response from the rest of the staff was "Thank God they're gone—they were always so negative."

I have since replaced the three who left. The interview process always begins in the break room, showing off the purple "Complaint Free World" wall and telling them this is a Complaint Free salon. *The three new replacements produce twice the income as the ones who left.*

Did you notice that the employees at the salon who complained the most were also the least productive? Perhaps it was their negative energy that repelled customers. More likely, however, they used their complaining to camouflage their poor work habits. They sought to blame their lack of productivity on the salon rather than themselves.

I was recently on a plane when I heard someone complaining to excuse poor performance. It was a large, full flight going from Kansas City, Missouri, to New York City. We had been sitting on the ground for quite a while without taking off; in fact, our departure time had long since come and gone. The travelers were starting to get agitated.

The flight attendant came on the PA system and announced,

"Ladies and gentlemen, we apologize for running late today but the Federal Aviation Administration mandates that flight crews have a certain amount of downtime between flights. Our flight crew got in late last night but they have met the mandatory requirement for rest time and are here now. We'll be getting off the ground soon."

> Ninety-nine percent of all failures come from people who have the habit of making excuses.
>
> —GEORGE WASHINGTON CARVER

People around me began to complain. Personally, I was thinking how lucky we were to get a pilot who was well rested.

Soon we were out on the tarmac ready for takeoff. The pilot said that we were next in line for takeoff and asked the flight attendants to take their seats. But then something happened. Or, I should say, *nothing* happened. We waited, waited, and waited. The pilot came back on the PA to say that they had discovered a problem with one of the jet's generators and we would have to return to the gate to have it repaired.

Again, people around me began to complain loudly to one another. All I could think of was how fortunate we were that they discovered this *on the ground.*

We didn't deplane but stayed aboard while they made the repair, which took over an hour. In time, I realized that I should have already landed in New York and needed to call my wife, Gail, because I always call her when I land. I dug out my cell phone and my call went something like this:

> Hi, it's me. No, as a matter of fact we haven't taken off yet. . . . Well, the flight crew got in late last night and so didn't have the necessary amount of FAA-required downtime to fly yet this morning. . . . Well, once they got here they discovered a problem with the plane. . . . Yes. . . . I don't know. . . . Soon, I hope. I'll call you when I get there. Love you. . . . Bye.

I was not complaining. I was stating facts. I was speaking without any negative, how-dare-they-do-this-to-me energy. However, in the seat directly in front of me, another man decided to call his wife. Here is what I heard as his end of their conversation:

> It's me . . . No! Of course not! . . . We haven't even taken off yet. . . . Well, the pilot, better known as Sleeping Beauty, got here late. . . . I know! . . . Then they discovered there was something wrong with this piece of s——t airplane. . . . What's going to happen? I'm going to miss my connection, that's what's going to happen. . . . I won't get to see the client! . . . The sale? The sale isn't going to happen; you can just forget about it. . . . Why? I told you! I'm not going to get to see the client, that's why! . . . How do I know? I know because *I'm going to miss my connection*! . . . Look, this was my one chance to see this client. . . . Yes, it's my only chance. Listen, I told you what's going to happen! I'll call you if I get there! Goodbye!

He was saying that all hopes of selling to this particular client whatever it was he said were gone because one flight was delayed. He was excusing his poor performance.

Prior to entering the ministry, I was in sales. For 20 years I sold advertising, cell phones, and insurance, among other things, and from my experience there is never only "one chance" to see any client. One postponed flight, however, and this poor guy had excused himself from making a sale.

The not-so-ironic thing that happened next is that the pilot came on the PA again. Addressing the more than 200 passengers on our plane, he said, "Ladies and gentlemen, we're sorry for the delay. We know it took quite a while to fix this issue but your safety is our primary concern. We're signing the paperwork on the repair now and we'll be taking off here in about ten minutes. And we've got good news for you. For those who need them, we've been able to arrange for connecting flights for everyone on board . . . except two people."

He then called the names of the two people who would not be reaching their intended destination this trip. And when he did, my salesman friend heard his name, leaped up, spluttered "Of course!" along with several expletives, grabbed his carry-on bag and stormed off the plane.

◈

Relationships are connections between people which bring up all sorts of interpersonal needs. When complaining is prevalent in a relationship, the griping is some combination of a need to <u>G</u>et attention, <u>R</u>emove themselves from responsibility, <u>I</u>nspire envy, establish <u>P</u>ower, and/or <u>E</u>xcuse poor performance.

But isn't it healthy to complain? We shouldn't keep things bottled up, right? Aren't we supposed to "get it out"? Isn't it healthy to vent? We'll explode this myth in the next chapter.

Opening Up

1. Make a list of the things you commonly complain about, then write down whether the motivation behind your complaints is to:

- <u>G</u>et attention
- <u>R</u>emove yourself from responsibility
- <u>I</u>nspire envy
- <u>P</u>ower
- <u>E</u>xcuse poor performance

Remember, your reasons may fall under multiple categories.

2. Look for patterns and journal about what you might say or do to get your needs met without resorting to complaining.

3. You are 100 percent able to change how you show up in a relationship and, thereby, change the dynamic of the relationship. Think of a relationship that you find challenging and make a list of things you might do to be the type of person where these issues would not present themselves.

CHAPTER 5

Getting It Out

It is only imperfection that complains of what is
imperfect. The more perfect we are, the more gentle
and quiet we become toward the defects of others.

—François de Fénelon

I n 2006 my wife, Gail, our daughter, Lia, and I spent Christmas at my mother-in-law's log cabin near Asheville, North Carolina. Shortly after our arrival we sat on the deck of the cabin gazing at the high mountain on the opposite side of the valley. Atop the mountain was an old fire tower. In previous trips to the cabin, we had tried, unsuccessfully, to hike to the top of the distant mountain, climb the fire tower, and take in the magnificent and expansive view it must surely provide.

In prior attempts we had made it as high as 70 percent of the way up the mountain but the sun would begin to set and, fearing being trapped in the cold, we had turned back. This time we resolved to make it. Nothing was going to stop us. We made plans to begin hiking early the next day and, come what may, we were going to reach the mountaintop and scale the fire tower.

We set out just after dawn for the trailhead. For December in the Great Smoky Mountains, it was a particularly beautiful day. There was hardly a cloud in the sky and the temperature inched up near 60 degrees. Knowing the weather would be favorable and we would work up a sweat while hiking, we wore only light sweaters and jeans.

About an hour into our trek we found that an ice storm had knocked down several large trees in our path. A few were stacked so high that we could not climb over the pile of timber; we had to take the long way around their ends. This led to our going on and off the trail several times but we managed to find our way back on track after only a little searching. When we felt lost, the fire tower loomed overhead like a lighthouse reminding us of our direction. As we climbed we talked, sang, and laughed.

Around noon we stopped for lunch, building a small fire by a creek. We roasted hot dogs and marshmallows. We talked about what it would be like to stop in this same spot on our way down to rest and compare notes about the splendid view we would have seen from the tower. Dousing the fire, we continued our trek but began to notice changes in the terrain we had not seen on previous hikes along this trail. In several spots we had to press our bodies against rock walls and shuffle sideways to avoid falling into deep holes. Every quarter mile or so we came upon a new large hole that had been formed when summer rains poured down the mountain and washed away portions of the trail. The holes were steep as cliffs and ranged in depth from a few feet to nearly twenty feet.

We reached one crevice that was so deep we had to veer considerably off the trail. The detour took us around the side of the mountain and out of sight of the tower. We repeatedly conferred as to whether or not we were going in the right direction and each time decided we were on track. We congratulated ourselves for making good time.

The trail eventually opened up and we were giddy with excitement, ready to celebrate having finally conquered the mountain. However, our revelry was short-lived. We discovered that the detour we had taken to avoid the last crevice had taken us up a different part of the mountain entirely. We were now considerably further away from our goal than we'd thought. We checked our watches and discussed the rationality of continuing. If any of us felt it might be a good idea to turn back, we kept quiet, as above us the fire tower beckoned. It seemed so close although we knew it wasn't. We hiked on.

The last 500 yards were the most difficult. We grabbed the trunks of small trees and pulled ourselves up the steep incline. Gaining a foothold proved difficult on the muddy ground beneath us. We jammed our hiking sticks into the earth like ice axes to keep from sliding down the incline. After many long hours of effort, exhausted and sweating, we found ourselves gasping for breath at the foot of the tower. We had made it! The view from where we stood was astounding. Once we ascended the tower, it became breathtaking.

We stood inside the abandoned tower for half an hour looking out in every direction and drinking in the beauty of the Smokies. We shot picture after picture of ourselves silhouetted against the waves of mountains beneath us.

At approximately 2:30 p.m. we began our descent. This would give us plenty of time to make it back to the cabin before sunset. The temperature had dropped noticeably from just a few hours before and we were thankful we had the exercise of hiking to keep us warm. The mountain is owned by a lumber company and the top portion had been clear-cut, making it easy for us to find a trail. But as we entered into the woods we had a feeling we were on the wrong path. A couple of times we doubled back to the treeless top of the mountain to get our bearings. Back and forth we walked, searching for the trail home.

It took the better part of an hour to find the right trail and we walked hastily to make up for lost time. Going down was faster and easier than coming up. We reached the spot where we'd eaten lunch earlier and agreed the view had been even better than we'd imagined. On we hiked. The temperature continued to drop. I watched the sun as it neared the "horizon." I put "horizon" in quotation marks because even though the sun was not supposed to set for another hour or so, because we were on the back side of one mountain and surrounded by other mountains, the landscape created a false horizon. The time of sunset according to the local news station was one thing; the sun going down behind the mountains ahead of us was another.

It seemed we went from full daylight to blackest night in a matter of moments. It was around five o'clock and we could not see inches in front of us. This was a day hike. We'd thought we'd be back by early afternoon and so we had not planned for this cave-like darkness. We had no flashlight and only the light clothes on our backs to stave off the ever-increasing cold. We began to shuffle our feet to feel for the path. We all agreed that we must have gotten off the trail and so we took a sharp turn to our right. Instantly we found ourselves trying to push through a wall of dense, spiny bushes. We could feel cuts opening on our hands and faces. We considered turning back but we were certain the correct path lay on the other side of the thicket, so we pressed on.

In a bizarre game of Marco Polo, we called out one another's names to try to stay together. Even though we were less than an arm's length apart, we could not see each other. Suddenly something jumped into my mind—the holes. In the inky blackness, even if we found the path we could fall into a crevice and get seriously hurt if not killed. "We've got to stop," I said.

"What do you mean, stop?" Gail said through chattering teeth. "I'm freezing. We've got to get home!"

I reminded her about the gaping holes that lay ahead. "We could fall into one of those and get hurt," I said. A feeling of desperation slammed down upon us all at once.

"What are we going to do?" asked Lia. "I'm really cold."

I pulled out my cell phone and dialed 911. "Call Failed" flashed upon the screen. Looking at my phone, I saw that I had no cell coverage.

"What *are* we going to do?" I wondered. We stood in silence until the blue light from my phone timed out, leaving us again in blackness. I pressed the keypad again and the blue light shone once more. In the darkness it provided about two feet of dim illumination. I drew in my breath and said softly, "We're going to have to stay here until morning. It's the only safe thing."

Nobody spoke for a minute or two, and I began to worry that Lia might get scared. "Lia," I said, "Mommy might get scared. I want you and mom to sit on the ground and hold hands."

"Then what?" she asked.

"Just keep telling Mommy it's going to be okay," I said.

The cell phone had a protruding knob on the back to click into a belt holster. I clenched the little stem between my front teeth so the screen faced out. I pressed the keypad and the pale light came on. I'll never forget the hazy blue image of my wife and our eight-year-old daughter holding hands while sitting on the icy ground, Lia's voice repeating reassuringly, "It's going to be okay, Mommy. It's going to be okay."

I got down on my hands and knees and felt around for the driest leaves. Finding some that were not too wet, I piled them up and then set out in search of wood to make a fire. The phone gave just enough light for me to gather whatever twigs and dead wood I could find. I piled the twigs on the leaves as Lia kept on task. "It's going to be okay, Mommy," she said, her words unsteady now as she shivered in the cold. Reaching into my pocket, I dug out a nearly empty pack of matches. I, too, was feeling the cold and my hands shook. I lit the first match and the spark flew off from the matchstick toward the ground, dying in flight. There were only a few matches left. The second match caught fire and I lit the leaves.

They began to smolder. Soon the twigs began to crackle and we had ourselves a fire.

I made ever-widening circles in the firelight to search for wood. After a couple of hours I had amassed a large, loosely packed pile of branches and limbs. "This will last us all night," I thought. I sat on the ground and put my arms around Lia. She was sitting close to the fire and although the front of her body felt warm, her back was like ice.

The only sounds to be heard were the crackling of the fire and groaning of our empty stomachs. "When we get back to Grandma's what are we going to have for breakfast?" I asked. The question allowed us to focus beyond the problem we found ourselves in and instead on its resolution—breakfast in our warm cabin.

Without a moment's hesitation Lia said, "Cinnamon toast and hot chocolate." Obviously she had been thinking about this very thing.

"Mmmm, that sounds delicious," Gail said, flashing me a smile that warmed my heart through the cold and gave me renewed hope. For the remainder of the night, we talked about how great the cinnamon toast and hot chocolate was going to be.

Lia fell asleep on the ground. From time to time, she whimpered softly. Soon I realized I had greatly misjudged the amount of wood we needed—the pile was nearly gone. I again put the cell phone in my mouth and went out in search for more.

Once I had another, even larger pile of limbs and sticks gathered, Gail and I decided to take turns feeding the fire while the other slept. I took first watch. Gail lay on the frigid ground next to Lia but never could get comfortable enough to doze off. After a couple of hours she took over the fire detail and I lay down to sleep. A half hour into my fitful rest, I awoke to see her standing over the fire, rocking back and forth, seemingly about to fall asleep standing up. She looked so brave and yet so fragile. On the ground next to me lay the most precious thing in my life—my only child.

It was during one of Gail's turns at fire watch that the sun finally peeked over the mountain we had summited so victoriously only the day before. After what seemed like the protracted darkness of an Alaskan winter, there was finally light. We roused Lia, who said, "Let's go get that cinnamon toast," and we began walking. We were indeed off the trail but not more than fifty feet.

After a few hours' hike, we savored several servings of cinnamon toast and hot chocolate before snuggling on the couch near the cabin's fireplace and falling asleep.

I share this true story to ask you some questions:

- How would our difficult situation have improved if we had complained to one another about our predicament?
- Would griping about the cold or our hunger have gotten us off the mountain faster?
- If one of us would have complained, would the others have felt comforted or more hopeful?

The answer to all of these is, of course, no. If we had griped about our situation, it only would have made the experience that much more challenging for us all.

> Venting your anger is not going to diminish it.
>
> Processing your anger will release your negative energy so you can move past it.

When it comes to being Complaint Free and enjoying Complaint Free relationships, I'm often asked some variation of the following: "Shouldn't I get out my anger? Isn't it healthy to vent?"

Anger is negative energy. You don't lose it by passing it on to other people. Rather, you raise *their* level of upset, which feeds on and compounds your own distress. Venting anger through complaining is not going to diminish upset; it is going to increase it. However, you can process challenging situations in a way that will help you find solutions you may not have seen on your own.

Venting

Most clothes dryers are vented. They have a long, wide vent hose that extends outside, safely removing excess heat created during the drying process. It would be healthy if we human beings could similarly vent our anger and frustration and release it forever. However, what most people call venting typically involves griping to other people. In loud and angry words, they tell how they have been wronged or disappointed. In doing this, they think they are "getting it out." They are not.

There is a common misconception that griping about a person or situation makes us feel better and releases stress, that somehow it cleanses the anger from us. It is believed that by telling another person how upset we are we can vent anger just as smoke would rise up a chimney and be gone forever. What most people call venting is actually complaining.

Venting is:

- Complaining. It is energetic statements focused on the problem at hand rather than the resolution sought.
- Done by a person to Get attention, Remove him or her from responsibility, Inspire envy or brag, have Power over someone, Excuse poor performance, or any combination thereof.
- About assigning blame to someone other than the person doing the speaking.

If "getting it out" means doing something physical to release the upset, then for some people this is indeed helpful. Some psychologists believe that it is cathartic for an angry person to punch pillows and break things to discharge negative energy. People who are prone to repressing their emotions may find this a help in expressing what they are feeling. Sigmund Freud recommended this tactic.

Others, however, disagree. A recent story reported on National Public Radio quotes psychologist Jeffrey Lohr of the University of Arkansas, who has reviewed decades of research on cathartic anger. Cathartic anger is a term used in psychological circles for expressing anger in a physical way such as yelling, punching a pillow, or breaking dishes. Lohr found that "punching pillows and breaking dishes doesn't reduce subsequent anger expression." In fact, it tends to have the opposite effect.

The best way to know whether punching a pillow or breaking something helps you to release your upset or only increases it is to try the technique and see how you feel later. It might help you to bring your anger to the surface so you can fully embrace how you are feeling. Note that Lohr is not saying that a person should suppress angry feelings; rather, they should speak them without getting emotional about them. (This is processing, and we will discuss processing in detail later.) But remember that this outward physical expression is always done with inanimate objects, such as punching a pillow or breaking a dish. *It is never done to or directed toward another person.*

Having and expressing feelings is normal and healthy for everyone. Projecting this upset at others is neither healthy nor beneficial to the person feeling the anger and it is damaging to the relationship because it raises the level of upset of the person hearing the rant.

When a person attempts to "get it out" by venting, sharing the upset with others, it tends to solidify and perpetuate the problem rather than lessen it. As the listeners hear the complaints, they will often reinforce what the person is saying with comments of their own that may amplify the person's upset. They think they are being "supportive" by agreeing and adding additional observations but what they are doing is like trying to extinguish a fire with gasoline.

When we vent, we are looking for validation for our victimhood. So we take our issues to the people who are most likely to agree that we have been wronged. The other person then offers additional validating comments that activate the "Dissatisfaction → Complaint" loop.

In a study published in the *Journal of Developmental Psychology*, researchers followed a group of 813 third through ninth graders in the Midwest for six months. The students were asked about whom they considered to be their closest friends and what they discussed most frequently. The results showed that girls who talked excessively to one another about their problems (vented) were more likely to experience symptoms of anxiety or depression. This, in turn, led to more talking about problems and negative feelings, which brought out more venting, which led to more dissatisfaction, which led to still more problems.

Consider this: if people were truly able to get out their negative emotions by venting them, wouldn't people who complain the most tend to be the happiest? Think of someone you know who complains frequently. How happy does that person seem to be? Chances are he or she tends to be pretty miserable.

> If people were able to get out their negative emotions by venting, wouldn't people who complain the most be the happiest?

We recently held our first annual Complaint Free Cruise. We took a luxurious ship from Fort Lauderdale, Florida, to Key West, then to the Grand Cayman Islands, and finally to Ocho Rios, Jamaica. People from across the United States and Canada came for seven days of fun, sun, sea, fine dining, dancing, excursions, and seminars on Complaint Free living. The service we received was top-notch, the food was delicious, and our time together was exquisite. However, one of our guests was in a cabin next to a couple who was *not* part of our group. In the midst of this paradise, this man and woman began to argue and their fighting escalated. Using harsh and angry words, they yelled at each other for extended periods of time. Finally their anger subsided (or, more likely, they ran out of energy), the fighting stopped, and their cabin became quiet.

If we are to believe that we can dissipate anger by sharing it with someone else, then this couple should have had a blissful time the rest of the cruise. Based on their shouting, they truly "got it out." Murray Straus, a sociologist in the field of family violence, finds that couples who yell at each other do not thereafter feel less angry but *more* angry. And the next night this couple was at it again until the ship authorities had to intervene.

Yelling does not make you less upset; it makes you more upset. Complaining does not improve the situation; it perpetuates it and makes you more dissatisfied by launching you into the "Dissatisfaction → Complaint" loop. You are not helping yourself or the relationship when you complain to another person. Rather, you are trying to get one of your interpersonal needs met, as noted by our acronym G.R.I.P.E. It is fine to get your needs met but attempting to do so by venting is going to have a damaging effect on the relationship. It is going to lower the energy of the other person and create a toxic environment.

Venting is often an attack on a person who is not present. It is an aggressive act and this aggression can be addictive. This explains why couples such as the one fighting on the cruise are *more* likely to argue and fight after having already done so. On the website Psych Central, Dr. Rick Nauert writes that the brain processes aggression the same way it processes drugs and alcohol. He quotes Craig Kennedy, a professor of special education and pediatrics: "We have found that the 'reward pathway' in the brain becomes engaged in response to an aggressive event and that dopamine is involved."

Dopamine is released when drug addicts are exposed to drugs and when alcoholics drink. When people act angrily or aggressively, dopamine is involved; they get a rush or "high" just like a drug addict or alcoholic that makes them crave more stimulation from additional aggressive experiences. This is common to all vertebrates.

Scientists conducted experiments with a pair of mice—a male and a female—that were housed in the same cage. In a nearby cage, five "intruder" mice were kept. The female mouse was temporarily removed, and an intruder mouse was introduced in her place. This caused an aggressive response by the male "home" mouse that included tail rattling, an aggressive sideways stance, boxing, and biting.

The home mouse was then trained to poke a target with its nose if it wanted the intruder to return. Every time the home mouse poked the target, an intruder was let into the home cage, at which point the home mouse would again behave aggressively. The target was presented to the home mouse once each day and *every time* it was presented the home mouse poked the target, inviting an intruder in. According to the author, the home mouse "experienced the aggressive encounter with the intruder as a reward."

So not only does venting not lessen our upset or improve our problems, but it can trigger something inside of us that makes us perceive conflict as a reward and seek to repeat it—we can get high on aggression.

Processing

> **Process:** a continuing development involving many changes, generally involving a number of steps

If you have an issue with someone, you can truly resolve it only by talking directly to that person. However, if an issue with someone is particularly challenging for you, it may be helpful to process with someone else before approaching the person you need to speak with. As the above definition explains, processing involves changes and—this is important: these changes are in *you,* not the person you are processing about and not the person you are processing with.

Processing is about working through something; it's seeking clarity where you may be unclear. Processing involves going dispassionately through the facts to make sure your energy is clear regarding the person or situation. It is not griping to validate your position. You are 50 percent of any relationship but you are 100 percent able to respond to improve the situation. Processing is making sure that you own the situation; it is discerning your options.

> Processing involves discerning changes *you* can make.

How can you tell when you are venting and when you are processing? The short answer is by your emotional energy. Do you feel charged up? Do you want to make the other person wrong and get someone to agree with you? Are you out to make the other person appear bad? Are you feeling angry or defensive? Are you poised for a fight? Do you want the person you are speaking with to join you in opposition to the person you are speaking about? If the answer to any of these is yes, you're venting, not processing.

To master processing, remember the acronym C.A.N. You CAN work through challenges and discover the best course of action for issues that are upsetting you by processing them with another person.

Complaint Free

About me, *not* someone else

Neutral story told to a neutral party

Complaint Free

If you are speaking to someone in an attempt to process an issue and you complain, you are venting, not processing. Remember, complaining is an energetic statement that focuses on the problem at hand rather than the resolution sought. If you want to run through a laundry list of what is being done to you and how unfair it is, then you are complaining.

This requires a great degree of personal honesty. If you are relating the information for any of the G.R.I.P.E reasons listed previously (Get attention, Remove yourself from responsibility, Inspire envy or brag, have Power over someone, or Excuse your poor performance), you are complaining, which means you are venting. You cannot complain your way to transformation, and *you* need to transform for the relationship to improve. The relationship exists only because you are part of it; changing you changes it.

> You cannot complain your way to transformation.

Your focus should be on resolving the situation. You should talk to the other person about how you would ideally like the issue to be once it is favorably resolved. And your intention should be for the best for *all* involved. Your ideal solution should not include the person you are challenged by being harmed or diminished—again, that's venting. Rather, it should be an ideal outcome, best for all.

If you are uncertain if you are complaining, go back and reread the detailed explanation of G.R.I.P.E in the previous chapter.

About Me

Processing is about changing the person doing the processing.

Let me say that again. Processing is about changing the person doing the processing. Processing is not about finger-pointing or assessing blame. It is asking, "What can I do differently to cause an improvement in the relationship?" It's realizing that you are 100 percent able to respond in the situation and delving into what you can do and how you can change to make things better.

In family dynamics psychology, instructors often use a mobile, one of those hanging pieces of sculpture that balances delicately based on the weight of its various pieces, to demonstrate how a change in one person changes the dynamic of all the relationships that person has. If you lift up on one part of a mobile, the weight shifts and every part of the mobile moves accordingly. The same is true in relationships, be they love relationships, families, or work relationships—if one person changes, the whole dynamic of the connection shifts. And you must be willing to be that person. You must be the one willing to make the change.

> How can I change and thereby cause the relationship to change?

As you process, the question becomes, "How can I change and, in so doing, cause the relationship to change?"

In 1955 Joseph Luft and Harry Ingham created a cognitive psychological tool known as the Johari window. ("Johari" is a joining of the first letters of Luft's and Ingham's first names.) To understand the Johari window, imagine a window with four panes. The first pane is that part of ourselves that we see and others see as well. The second pane is that part of us that we see and others do not see—our private thoughts, dreams, fears, and aspirations. The third pane holds those aspects of ourselves that we do not see but others do. And the fourth pane is that part of us that is not experienced or understood by ourselves or by other people.

Processing involves an attempt to understand and embrace the third pane of the Johari window—those aspects of ourselves that others see but which we do not. When we process a situation with someone, we are seeking understanding as to how we are present-

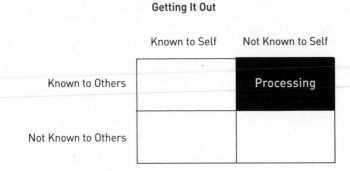

Johari Window

ing in the relationship. It is an attempt to understand our part in the situation. We cannot change what we cannot acknowledge and our ego mind often seeks to blind us to our part in a situation. Our ego wants us to believe that the other person is the total cause of the problem and we are helpless victims. So long as we have this perspective, we cannot change and the relationship becomes stuck.

When we process a situation, we ask, "What can I do differently to improve things?"

As you excavate, it is important that you *not* embrace what you discover about yourself as flaws. Don't get caught up in identifying yourself as flawed. *What you find out about yourself are not flaws—they are typically correctable behaviors.* Processing is not about assigning blame to the other person nor is it about assigning blame to yourself. Assigning blame removes any hope that the situation will improve. It writes the situation off as irresolvable.

Talking with someone and gaining agreement that your boss is a jerk is not processing and removes your ability to improve your work situation. "He's a jerk, period, end of discussion, live with it" gives you nowhere to go; you are stuck. But in a limitless universe you can never be stuck. Similarly, if you pigeonhole yourself as inherently flawed, you destine yourself to having the relationships of a flawed person. If, for example, you believe, "People are never honest with me," this belief solidifies your position as fact and dooms you to dishonest relationships.

Sharing your beliefs about how you have been wronged by another person or how you are a victim of someone else's behavior causes you to have the relationships you believe you, as a victim, deserve. And sharing your perspective of being a victim reinforces your being one.

In his book *Influence: The Psychology of Persuasion,* Robert B. Cialdini tells of an experiment where a researcher showed volunteers two lines and asked each person to decide which line was longest. One group of participants was asked to make their decision mentally and not tell anyone. Another group was instructed to write their conclusion on a pad which they could then erase without showing the answer to anyone. The third group of volunteers was asked to write down their answer and share it with the experimenter.

In a limitless universe, you can never be stuck.

Next, all of the participants were told that their answer was wrong; they were told they had not selected the longer line. They were then given a chance to change their mind. The participants who had shared their answer with another person (the experimenter) were the *least* willing to consider that they were incorrect. They stuck to their belief that the line they had chosen was indeed the longer of the two even though they had been told it was not.

When you talk to someone and describe yourself or someone with whom you share a relationship as flawed, you condemn the relationship to failure because it is built on a flawed foundation. A relationship is like a cake. If you bake a cake and one of the ingredients you use is rancid, the resulting cake will be unsavory. When you declare yourself or the other person to be beyond hope of improvement, you look for proof that your conclusion is correct, and in looking for proof, you find it again and again.

The power of this was demonstrated to me by two friends in Seattle, Washington. We had gone to a fine-dining restaurant for lunch. Even though we had been seated for more than ten minutes, our waiter had not acknowledged our presence. He walked right past us several times without welcoming us or taking our order.

What would you do in this situation? You might be tempted to think any or all of the following:

> "What the hell is wrong with this idiot? Can't he see we're sitting right here?"
>
> "He's ignoring me because I'm black [white, short, tall, thin, heavy, bald, have too much hair, whatever]."
>
> "If the waiter is this rude, the food is probably going to be lousy, too."

When you declare yourself or the other person to be beyond hope of improvement, you look for proof that your conclusion is correct, and in looking for proof, you find it again and again.

Rather than allowing the waiter's behavior to upset them, my friends went over and introduced themselves to the waiter while he stood entering another customer's order into the service computer. They told him we were ready to order and thanked him for stopping by soon. Instead of defining the waiter as substandard and then looking at every turn for evidence to corroborate their belief, they treated him with respect and appreciation.

When the waiter arrived at our table, his attitude was surly, though not, I believe, because my friends had fetched him, it just seemed he was having a bad day. As he went to get our drink order, my friends decided to launch themselves on a mission to get him to smile. Every time the waiter came to the table, which he began to do with much greater frequency, my friends smiled warmly at him, thanked him, and, where appropriate, complimented him. In short order, we were being well cared for by a smiling and genial server. My friends' behavior transformed him rather than cementing our relationship with him as negative and hopeless.

Placing blame negates your ability to be an agent for change in the relationship. I know of two women who in the past were in relationships with men who cheated on them. Both were understandably upset. One chose to define herself as a victim and continues to find herself in unsatisfying, unfaithful relationships, whereas the other established a standard of acceptable behavior in future romances.

After discovering the infidelity, the first woman went out of her way to tell all of her friends about the affair. She gained attention and sympathy by telling her story to anyone who would listen. She found that in relating her narrative she drew to her other women who had been cheated on, which reinforced her position as she grew into a belief that "all men cheat." She is currently in a relationship with a man who she thinks has been faithful so far, but as she told me, "There is no such thing as a monogamous man; it's just a matter of time."

> Placing blame negates your ability to be an agent for change in the relationship.

The other woman resolved to only be in relationships that were monogamous and asked herself what she could do in future romances to ensure this. She has now been married for nearly two decades and so far both she and her husband have remained faithful. Rather than looking for a monogamous man, she *chose* monogamy.

This second woman presents the best of herself to lessen her husband's temptation to look around for pleasure. She exercises regularly to stay fit and attractive. She is well groomed and dresses well to make certain she remains physically appealing to him. If she has challenges with her husband, she talks to him rather than complaining to or about him. (Remember the *Men's Health* article that found that men who cheat are often in complaining relationships?) She puts their intimate relationship high on her priority list to make certain they have frequent and enjoyable sex.

She talks with him to make certain he is satisfied and if he has feedback as to how their romantic life can improve, she doesn't take offense, she listens. Further, she takes responsibility for communicating her physical needs to him.

Most important, she decided in her mind that the man who cheated on her was not representative of all men; he was one, flawed man. This woman has made it clear to her husband that monogamy is the only option. As they compared previous love relationship histories early in their time together, she told him about her boyfriend who had cheated.

"What did you do?" he asked.

"I tossed him out and never had any further contact with him," she said.

"If I ever cheated on you, would you still love me?" he asked.

"Of course I'd still love you," she said. "I'd also miss you—because you'd be gone."

Her husband understood her message: "You cheat—you're gone." No threats. No "This is your last chance." One time and it's over! It doesn't matter if they have children together. It doesn't matter if their finances are intermeshed; if he has a sexual relationship with another person, it's over. This woman chose to have a monogamous relationship and takes responsibility for doing everything she can to ensure it happens, and so far it has.

In relationships you have choices that you may have never explored, and processing with another person lets you consider options you may not yet see. Processing invites you to look inside your Johari window and see how your behavior may be contributing to the challenge.

When you ask for feedback through processing, you must be willing to listen to the observations the other person offers. You must be open to hearing some things about yourself that you probably do not want to hear. There is a reason that these things lie in the third pane of the Johari window—they are aspects of yourself you do not see because, oftentimes, they are things you do not *want* to see. They seem like big, frightening issues or flaws and you have avoided them. Hearing that they exist may make you feel threatened. No one likes to hear he or she has been culpable in a difficult relationship.

Therefore, when you receive this information, take a deep breath. Know that your ego mind is—not *may, is* going to take offense. It may tell you that the person you are processing with is crazy, vindictive, or mean. This is normal. Just breathe through it.

If you respond to your processing partner with "What do you mean, I'm doing that and I'm the problem? How dare you say that!" this person will probably not help you process issues in the future. If you come back with negative and challenging energy, your partner will probably backpedal and withdraw or soften his or her observation, which does not serve you. Whether your partner states it or not, he or she will understand that you are looking for validation, not improvement, and you will lose this wonderful opportunity to reconstruct yourself and the relationship in the process.

Neutral

Processing is stating the facts—or at least your version of the facts. It is sharing what happened, when, and where. *Why* something happened is rarely neutral because when we get into *why* something happened we are making up a story about another's motives, which are often unknowable. Trying to explain why something happened leads to assigning blame.

Processing is just the facts. Processing does not get into conjecturing about motives or spotlighting another person's imperfections. Processing is like a news story that tells simply what happened. There is no commentary or analysis. When we process something with someone we tell the other person what happened as dispassionately as possible.

For example, you might process with someone about your day, "When Carl came into the office today he told us that some of our staff might be downsized and I've got to tell you I'm worried." This is stating the facts: Carl came into the office, Carl warned about potential downsizing, and the speaker admits being concerned. That's processing.

> When we get into *why* something happened we are making up a story about another's motives which are often unknowable. Trying to explain why something happened leads to assigning blame.

Venting would be, "Carl is such a lowlife jerk! I think he actually enjoys scaring us. He came strutting into the office today and told everyone that some of us are going to get fired. He could have at least prepared us, but no, not Carl! He doesn't care about anyone but himself. His job is safe—he's the boss's golden boy. But the rest of us? Well, who cares about us, right? We're just cogs in a machine. I'll probably be the first one let go and won't Carl just love that?"

These words are hardly neutral. There are facts here but they are interwoven with a narrative about Carl's motives and attacks on Carl's character. This account was told in order to elicit one or several G.R.I.P.E. responses.

When you process with someone, it doesn't mean you disregard your feelings. In fact, one of the important parts of processing a situation is acknowledging how you truly feel. Noted British author and statesman Benjamin Disraeli wrote, "Never apologize for showing feeling . . . when you do so you apologize for truth." When something happens and you feel sad, own your sadness. If something happens and you feel angry, profess your anger. If you are afraid, it's all right to admit you are afraid. You do so like this:

"I feel sad."

"I feel angry."

"I am afraid."

Naming and admitting your feelings brings them out of the shadows into the light so they can dissipate. Many people think they are expressing their feelings when they yell and shout. If you need to yell and shout, you may be one of those people who benefits from punching a pillow or screaming in the woods; again, this energy must always be directed toward an inanimate object and never another person. When you are speaking to a person, you don't lessen your upset by using an upset tone of voice.

> Never apologize for showing feeling . . . when you do so, you apologize for truth.
> —BENJAMIN DISRAELI

In their paper "The Angry Voice: Its Effects on the Experience of Anger and Cardiovascular Reactivity" Aron Wolfe Siegman, Robert A. Anderson, and Tal Berger detail a study they conducted on the impact of voice styles when discussing different situations. Men and women were asked to speak of either anger-arousing or neutral events using three different voice styles: (1) their normal voice, (2) a style that was fast and loud, or a (3) slow and soft style.

In describing the anger-arousing events—things that upset them—both male and female participants reported feeling significantly *more* angry and showed significantly *higher* blood pressure and heart rate reactivity when using a fast-loud voice style as compared with their normal voice. When they used a slow-soft voice style, they reported feeling significantly *less* angry and showed significantly *lower* blood pressure than when they used their normal voice.

Processing is neutral. It is the facts presented in a neutral way. The person with whom you process must also be a neutral party. If you are having a problem with your boss, rarely is another person in your department a neutral party. If you are having an issue with a family member, other family members tend not to make good processing partners. The person with whom you process is there to listen and reflect; he or she needs to be emotionally removed from the situation. He or she is there to listen for the facts, reflect back how you might be contributing to the situation, and invite you to explore options for improving things.

A processing partner should be a person who is:

- Someone you trust implicitly
- Neutral in the situation
- Able to stay above the conflict
- Able to just listen and reflect
- Truly interested in helping you
- Willing to tell you the unvarnished truth
- Someone from whom you are willing to hear the unvarnished truth

Because I am a minister, people often come to me for what is called spiritual counseling. We begin and end the sessions with prayer, which covers the spiritual part, but the counseling is often processing. They need a neutral, safe person to whom they can lay out a situation, discuss their feelings, and ask for help to see how they might change to make the situation better. A good psychologist will provide a place to process as a part of therapy. But you needn't speak to a minister or a therapist.

Find a friend or family member who is *NOT*:

- Involved in the situation
- Someone with a penchant for melodrama
- Going to try to make your issue about him or her
- Going to tell anyone else what you have shared

- Someone you are having a challenge with who may use what you share as ammunition to validate his or her position

It is important to believe that the person you are processing about actually had a positive intention behind his or her behavior. This is not easy to grasp, but to process the experience, this understanding is vital. The person's behavior may have been rude, it may have created conflict, it may even have been reprehensible, but at some level it was done in an attempt to create a good outcome for the person and/or others.

You need to embrace that this person had a positive intention in mind for what he or she did. The person's intention may have been deep-seated and complex; it may have been something the person was not fully aware of; it may have been done to get an interpersonal need met that you cannot fathom. The bottom line is, you must assume that there is a positive intention for the other person's actions or else you make him or her out to be an ogre and yourself to be a helpless victim. And the purpose of processing is to remember the truth that you are *not* a victim.

In *Anger: The Misunderstood Emotion,* author Carol Tavris tells of a study in which third-grade children expressed frustration and irritation with another child whom the experimenters had enlisted in helping with the experiment. The kids were given one of three ways of handling their anger. Some were permitted to talk it out with the adult experimenters, some were allowed to play with toy guns for "cathartic release," and some were given a reasonable explanation from adults as to the cause of the other child's annoying behavior.

Of the three options, which do you think best lowered the child's level of upset? It wasn't talking about it. It wasn't playing with toy guns—this made them *more* hostile and aggressive. The most successful way of dispelling the upset child's anger was to understand *why* the other child had behaved as he or she did (for example, "She was sleepy," "She was upset," "She was not feeling well," etc.). By understanding that the other child had a reason behind his or her actions, the upset child was best able to let the issue go. Rather than creating a reason why the other child acted in such a manner, the offended children were given a reason for the other child's behavior, and as a result, they became less upset.

A person with whom you are upset has a reason for his or her behavior, some positive intent. Just being willing to consider this makes you feel better, lowers your defenses, and opens you up to consider options you might explore and employ.

You feel negative energy in a relationship because you feel you do not have options—but you do. You feel stuck; you're not. Processing with a neutral third party takes the emotion out of the issues and makes the situation a puzzle to be solved rather than a hopeless quandary.

Remember, the underlying question in processing is always *"How can I change and, in so doing, cause the relationship to change?"* Finding answers to this question immediately frees you from feeling stuck; it energizes you and moves you forward toward a resolution.

Once you have discerned the best course of action then you must take it. You must be courageous enough to do what you feel guided to do to improve the relationship. Aristotle said, "Men acquire a particular quality by constantly acting a particular way . . . you become just by performing just actions, temperate by performing temperate actions, brave by performing brave actions." As you act like the person for whom the relationship would be ideal, you change, and in so doing, you change the dynamics and course of the relationship.

> You feel upset in a relationship because you think you don't have options— but you do.

Opening Up

1. You are 50 percent of any relationship but 100 percent able to choose how you will be in that relationship. What common challenges do you experience in your relationships? How would a person who does not have these challenges act in his or her relationships? How might you adjust to improve things?

2. The next time you are relating a stressful incident to someone, try to use a low, slow tone of voice as opposed to a loud, rapid tone. Journal about how you felt as a result of this exercise.

3. Before the need arises, decide who might be a good processing partner and invite that person to help you sort through challenges that arise. Share with him or her the ground rules for processing discussed in this chapter. Explain that you don't want validation or agreement; you want feedback about how *you* can grow and improve.

4. When you process, make note of the things that you might try to improve in your relationships. Share the results with your processing partner and ask for further insights.

CHAPTER 6

The Primary Relationship

*Since you must spend so much time with your-
self you might as well get some satisfaction out of
the relationship.*

—NORMAN VINCENT PEALE

"Why am I here?"

For millennia, human beings have wrestled with this question. The reason for our existence has been posed, pondered, and postulated around the world and throughout history.

Before I share my answer to this question, let's reflect on the question itself. Humanity's enduring quest to understand why we exist presupposes one thing—that people do, in fact, exist for a reason. What would spur this universal search to answer a question if we did not at our core know that the question had an answer? At some level it is coded into our genetic makeup that we are here for a reason, but for what reason?

> Relationships
> are for:
>
> 1. Fun
> 2. Growth

My answer to this question is simple: we are here to have fun and to grow.

We are here to have fun. Life is filled with wonderful experiences to dazzle our every sense. There are delightful things to smell, see, hear, touch, and taste: the smell of a chocolate cake baking, the delicious taste of that cake still warm from the oven and covered in thick, gooey icing, the lilting sound of children laughing, the breathtaking sight of a double rainbow after a summer rain, the exquisite tactile feel of petting a beloved pet. There are things everywhere that are fun. We might categorize these things with any of a number of terms, such as *pleasurable, exhilarating, tasty, satisfying, stimulating,* or *whatever,* but the bottom line is they are fun and if we were not embodied we could not experience them. Our bodies are more than housing for our souls; they are portals through which we experience pleasure.

The fun aspects of life are, I believe, intended to keep us in the game so we can engage in the primary reason for life, which is growth. The wonderful, fun, sensorial experiences make us want to continue to live so we can grow. Growth comes through facing challenges and adapting as a result. A bodybuilder knows that to grow muscle he has to pump iron until his muscles fail; when he has reached the outer limit of a muscle's current capacity, only then will the muscle grow. He must challenge the muscle to grow by pushing it to its current level of failure.

We experience soul growth in the same way, by pushing ourselves to our current level of failure. Rather than lifting weights, however, our souls grow by experiencing challenging situations and we develop the capacity to grow through them. If growth comes through challenges, experiencing a mixture of fun and growth is important. If our lives were nothing but these challenges, if our lives did not offer the savory pleasures of being alive, many would quit the game prematurely. In short, if life was all problems that led us to grow and no fun, who'd want to live?

Ray Kroc, founder of McDonald's, acknowledged the nature of growth when he said, "As long as you're green, you're growing, as soon as you're ripe, you're ready to rot." Life is about growth. Our bodies grow from the moment we are conceived. We may max out at a certain height but our body grows new cells as long as we are alive. Further, and far more significant, we continue to grow at an emotional and spiritual level. Throughout our lives we experience events that may be problematic and upsetting to us and from them we then learn new skills to overcome similar situations in the future. That's growth.

Growth is not easy; that's why we have pleasures to keep us here and moving through challenges that allow us to grow. Growth is nearly always uncomfortable. Growth is launching into uncharted, and therefore frightening, waters. Novelist Henry Miller wrote, "All growth is a leap in the dark, a spontaneous unpremeditated act without benefit of experience."

It could be said that life is like school. The difference is that in school you get a lesson and then you take the test, whereas in life (and relationships) you take the test and then you get the lesson. Life is always bringing us lessons. First we experience the test and then, if we are open and willing, we get the lesson and needn't take that particular test again. A similar situation may show up later but we will be able to handle it with ease. Why? Because we have grown and are now capable of dealing with the issue.

> In school you get the lesson and then take the test.
>
> In relationships you take the test and then you get the lesson.

We are here to grow and life experiences provide us with the impetus to do so. And, far from being just painful challenges, these experiences often come bearing gifts. Many who have found their niche in life and have greatly inspired and served others have done so because of, not in spite of, their life challenges. Many people who have meaningful and satisfying relationships today have had challenging and problematic relationships in the past. They have grown and gained new understanding as a result.

Why are we here? We are here to grow.

The laboratory for personal growth is relationships. Relationships call up things that are unhealed and provide us with the impetus and opportunity to work through them. To the extent that we work through what presents itself, we are able to move past the issue at hand. However, as long as we are alive, we never reach the end of this ongoing development. There is no "once and for all" when it comes to growth. The author Gertrude Stein once said, "There is no there there." As we discover issues about ourselves and grow through them, we can find satisfaction in their completion but as long as we're alive the lessons will continue. Every relationship provides opportunities for us to grow.

Growth never stops. People who seem the most youthful in their older years are the ones who continue to embrace change and growth. Relationships are the catalyst and the proving ground for our individual growth.

> We are here to grow and other people provide us with the challenges, the feedback, the role models, and the inspiration to do so.

I began this book by saying that relationships are not a want, they are a need—they are not optional. Everyone needs connections with other people, and this is the reason. We are here to grow and other people provide us with the challenges, the feedback, the role models, and the inspiration to do so.

When it comes to romantic relationships, a term that gets bantered around frequently is "soul mates." Some people embrace the idea that each person has one and only one soul mate. The two somehow complete each other. They are like a unique lock and key that will only work with each other, and life is about searching, finding, and being with that one and only true love. When you find this one person, your mission is complete and you then bask forever in the warm glow of an idyllic relationship.

This idea may sell a lot of Disney movies and Lifetime television specials but these films and programs rarely show what happens after Cinderella and Prince Charming ride off on their majestic steed.

What happens? Life happens. Issues come up. Problems arise. Idiosyncrasies emerge and are wrongly categorized as faults. In short, all hell breaks loose. When this happens, the two "soul mates" are perplexed.

"How could there be trouble in paradise?" they wonder. "How could we have issues with each other? We're soul mates!" The two begin to wonder if they made a mistake. Perhaps they are not, in fact, soul mates. Maybe they are with the wrong person. Maybe someone *else* is their soul mate. Having considered this option, their minds begin seeking and finding supporting data that they are not perfectly bound at a soul level; soon they begin to emotionally drift apart and may eventually physically separate.

Couples who are searching for their one and only soul mate often want the fun without the growth. Sorry, Cindy and Prince C.; it doesn't work that way. Relationships are about growth.

Relationships are fun. There is the connection of sharing your dreams and aspirations with someone. There is inspiration the other person provides. There is laughter. There is the aesthetic appreciation of each other. There is the enjoyment of shared activities. There is the thrill of creating new things together. There is the satisfaction of overcoming challenges together. There are adventures to be explored. And in intimate relationships there is sex. All of which I would categorize as fun. In fact, as comedian Woody Allen quipped about sex, "That was the most fun I've had without laughing."

Relationships bring us fun. Relationships bring us growth. And growth comes through challenges. There is the challenge of learning to effectively communicate your needs to another person; the challenge of understanding someone else's moods; the challenge of not being threatened by another person's need for independence; the challenge of accepting the other person's way of doing things as different but no less legitimate than your own; and so on. Relationships touch off everything about us that we need to address. *And that's what they are intended to do.*

The concept of soul mates is flawed in that it implies that every person is somehow incomplete and needs someone else who is also incomplete to join with in order to be complete. Successful relationships are ones in which both people are complete in themselves whether they are in a relationship or not. Complete people do not feel somehow lacking without another person in their lives. They do not define themselves by their relationship. They understand that they *want* a relationship, but they aren't obsessed with being completed by another. Two halves don't make a whole—two halves make a mess of the relationship.

Am I saying that I disagree with the concept of soul mates? Absolutely not. I believe completely and unreservedly in soul mates. In fact, I believe you have six billion soul mates.

Everyone on earth is your soul mate. If a soul mate is someone who completes you, someone with whom you are connected at a deep spiritual level, then even the most casual of acquaintances is connected with you and provides you with this opportunity. Everyone you meet brings up things that will complete you if you are open to them. Your interactions with others bring up things you need to heal.

Don't assume based on what we have presented thus far that you must remain in relationships that do not serve you. Depending on the parameters of the relationship, the other person may simply not be a fit. If you are an employer and you hire someone unwilling to perform the duties detailed in the job description, then you need to release that employee. If you are in an intimate relationship and monogamy is important to you, a person who cheats on you has got to go.

> Much of your pain is self-chosen.
> —KAHLIL GIBRAN

In my previous book *A Complaint Free World,* I shared that my first wife left me after seven years of marriage. The experience devastated me because I had bought into this cultural myth of a single soul mate for everyone. I felt that she was my "one and only" and, having lost her, I was certain the rest of my life would be void of love and companionship.

Further, my parents divorced when I was in my teens and I had vowed never to divorce. So when my first wife said she no longer wished to be married, I felt like a failure. I called my dear friend René to help me process the breakup of our marriage. He gave me advice that raised my spirits and helped me through the pain I was feeling. He said, "Will, perhaps you might stop looking at the end of your relationship as a failure. Instead, you might consider that the relationship is complete and no longer needs to continue."

Wow. What a paradigm shift. I wasn't a failure because our relationship ended. Our relationship had not failed; it was complete.

If you think that you failed in your previous relationships, you carry a person who is a "relationship failure" (you) into future relationships. You are putting an unsavory ingredient into the recipe and the result will be unpalatable. Your past relationships did not fail; they were complete. And if you got the lessons that were presented in a relationship, you needn't worry about them manifesting in your current relationships.

If, however, you go from relationship to relationship and discover the same problems, it simply means there is something that you have yet to recognize, own, and heal. And right where you are is the best place to do this. "Heal" means to return to wholeness; challenges in relationships provide an opportunity to return to your innate wholeness.

There is a botanical principle known as *phototropism.*

Phototropism says that many plants grow in the direction of sunlight. If you have such a plant, it will not grow well and be healthy if you do not occasionally turn it toward the light. It will grow off balance and the side of the plant that is in the shade will wither and die. You must turn the dark side toward the light for the plant to grow. The same is true for you. You must turn your inner challenges toward the light. Once they are in the light, you can see them. Once they are in the light you can address them. Once they are in the light you can heal them. Relationships turn you toward the light by bringing up your "stuff."

In every relationship, there are actually four relationships occurring simultaneously:

1. **Your relationship with the other person**—the stories you tell yourself about them, the pictures you hang in your mind about them, the things that attract you to them, the needs they fulfill for you, and the things you find appealing about them.

2. **Their relationship with you**—the stories they tell themselves about you, the pictures they hang in their mind about you, the things that attract them to you, the needs you fulfill for them, and the things they find appealing about you. The other person's relationship with you is quite different from your relationship with them.

3. **Your relationship with yourself**—the stories you tell yourself about yourself, the pictures you hang in your mind about yourself, the things you find appealing about yourself. All the attributes of a relationship between two people exist and are ongoing within each person's relationship with him- or herself.

4. **The other person's relationship with him- or herself**—the other person, too, holds a unique perspective on him- or herself—telling stories about him- or herself, hanging men-

tal pictures, appreciating some things and challenged by other things about him- or herself.

Each of these relationships is unique and based on individual perspectives. If you want to improve your relationship with someone, you can because you have the power to positively transform three of these four relationships.

Best-selling author Peter McWilliams wrote, "All relationships are with yourself—and sometimes they involve other people. The most important relationship in your life—the one you have, like it or not, until the day you die—is with yourself."

The first relationship you must heal is your relationship with yourself. The common ingredient in all of your relationships is you. When your relationship with yourself is made whole it has a cascading effect in your relationships with others, who will begin to experience you in a more positive way. When your relationship with yourself is put on a solid foundation, you find it easier to relate to others. Rather than other people being a projection of your unresolved issues, you will begin to see them with fresh eyes. Then, by utilizing the principles we have discussed, you can build bridges of understanding and mutual collaboration.

> Your ability to get along with other people is a reflection of your ability to get along with yourself.

All relationships with others are ultimately a reflection of your relationship with yourself. Your ability to get along with other people is a reflection of your ability to get along with yourself. If you are angry with yourself, you will be angry with other people. If you are a perfectionist with yourself, you will be a perfectionist with others. If you are gentle and loving with yourself, you will be gentle and loving with others.

If you think that you are "worthless," "lazy," "stupid," or "unsuccessful," you are going to attract people to you who support this belief system. If you are surrounded by people who do not think highly of you, chances are you do not think highly of yourself. You feel that you deserve the treatment others are giving you because it's reflective of how you treat yourself. People who value themselves will not allow others to treat them poorly. Best-selling author Don Miguel Ruiz said that we will not tolerate being with anyone who treats us worse than we treat ourselves.

To achieve Complaint Free relationships, you must take responsibility for *all* of your relationships. You are responsible, therefore, for your relationship with yourself and you are able to positively transform this relationship. I will provide some exercises to help you through this process.

Remember, working through your relationship with yourself is not optional. You can either do this work intentionally, with the exercises we are about to discuss, or by experiencing problems in your relationships, which will continue and amplify until you get the lesson. You will repeat test after test until you get the lesson. If you'll invest the time to do the exercises, you can work through your relationship with yourself, improve your relationships with others, and lessen the frequency and severity of life's tests.

> To achieve Complaint Free relationships, you must take responsibility for *all* of your relationships.

To do these exercises, you'll want to get a journal, notebook, or several sheets of paper. Commit to a half hour or so each day for the next week to ten days. These exercises have a compounding effect when done sequentially and daily, so give this gift to yourself.

"What?" you may be thinking. "I'm too busy. Where am I going to find thirty minutes for each of the next ten days?"

According to research, the average adult spends more than five hours *every day* watching television. Many adults spend two hours or more per day on the Internet. So if you watch TV or surf the Web, you've got time. If you are serious enough about your relationships to buy this book, you can carve out a half hour. Take responsibility and be honest with yourself that you *do* have the time and make the effort. So grab a pen and paper—now—and let's get started with:

1. WHAT ARE YOU RELATING ABOUT YOURSELF?

Relate is the root of *relationship* and it means "to recount or to tell."

EXERCISE 1. What do you tell yourself about yourself? What words do you use to describe yourself? Write out as many descriptive words about you as come to mind.

Write "I am . . ." at the top of a page and let the words flow. You might be surprised to find out what comes up but it is important to know what you think of yourself because your relationships are going to be an outpicturing of the thoughts you hold about yourself. Include not only the things that are challenging about yourself but also your many positive attributes. Keep digging; they're there.

Next, turn the page over and, again, write the words "I am . . ." at the top of the page. Then list all the ways you would *like* to be. Copy all of the positive attributes from the other side of the paper and then add all the glowing qualities you wish you possessed. Keep writing. Once you think you've written every positive attribute you can think of, put the paper somewhere private but easily accessible. Make a commitment to read only the side of the paper that lists the way you wish to become *every day* as you arise in the morning and before going to sleep each night. As more good qualities come to mind, add them to the list. Say aloud, "I am . . ." and then begin to say aloud what you are as your ideal self. As you read, imagine you already are the person you are reading about.

And—*this is the key to the whole exercise*—begin to look for proof that you do, in fact, have these attributes as you go about your day. Try to find evidence of at least one of these positive traits being expressed by you every single day.

EXERCISE 2. What stories have you told yourself about yourself? Write out key experiences in your life, stories and events that you feel define you. Specifically, think of times when you fell short of your ideal self.

Now, imagine that you are looking at these narratives with the eyes of limitless compassion. Consider each of these stories from the point of view of someone who loves you unconditionally. How might this loving person see you in this situation—as bad, or as someone who was attempting to get his or her needs met but lacked the resources and/or support to do so in a constructive way? How might you change the stories you have told yourself about yourself when you view them with the eyes of understanding and compassion?

Rewrite these stories, one by one, from this perspective and feel how the discomfort you have carried shifts to appreciation for yourself. When your mind drifts to these stories, remember them in the more positive and affirming way that you now know to be true.

2. WHAT PICTURES HAVE YOU HUNG IN YOUR MIND ABOUT YOURSELF?

Based on the events that have occurred in your life, you probably have some snapshots you call up about your journey. What images have you posted in your relationship with yourself? When you think about yourself, you may call to mind images of events that were embarrassing, unhappy, disheartening, problematic, stressful, or painful, limiting your ability to appreciate who you are.

It's time to change these pictures. Think of times when things have gone well for you. Write them down. Better still, if you have actual photos from happy and successful times, pull them out and attach them to your journal or post them where you can see them. Let these be the images you think of when you think of yourself. If you are going into a potentially challenging situation, close your eyes and call to mind images of times when you handled a similar situation well. Feel the feelings of having a similar, successful experience this time.

3. Don't confuse idiosyncrasies with flaws.

You are unique in the entire world and for all time. Because you are so intimately aware of your internal fears and judgments it is tempting to look at your distinct self as somehow flawed when compared to others. This happens because we tend to idealize those we admire and think they don't have painful insecurities or limiting behaviors, but such is not the case.

Personal strengths tend to have a corresponding downside. If you are outgoing, you may at times be perceived as overbearing. If you are by nature shy and reserved, some may see you as distant. If you are a person who is good at following things logically to a conclusion, you may find that abstract thought is challenging for you. If you have the gift of being a visionary and seeing the potential in people and situations, your focus may be so far in the future that you have a problem with day-to-day activities.

Your gifts are exactly that: gifts. Ask yourself whether you would be willing to give up the gifts you have to lessen the shadow they cast. Probably not.

A while back, my wife, Gail, and our daughter, Lia, who normally have a great relationship, were sniping at each other. Gail would say something and Lia would take what she said as a personal attack. Lia would make a comment and Gail took her statement as a slight. Their misperceptions created a loud back-and-forth dialogue. The tension in our house was palpable.

I finally asked both of them to sit down at the kitchen table. They each grabbed a seat at opposite ends of the table as far from the other as possible. I handed each of them a pen and a piece of paper and asked them to do an exercise. "Gail," I said, "I want you to imagine that Lia has died suddenly." At first Gail looked at me with shock, a look that soon faded into defiance. "Just give this a try," I said. "I know you both love and appreciate each other and I think that you've somehow lost that today, so just give this a try, okay?" Gail nodded reluctantly.

"Okay," I continued, "for the purpose of this, Lia has tragically died. The funeral is tomorrow and I need you to write out a eulogy for her funeral." Gail continued to stare at me. "Consider this to be your one chance to tell the world all the wonderful things you admire and value about her."

Our eyes locked. After a moment, Gail looked down quietly and began to make notes on the page. Lia smiled triumphantly, thinking I was siding with her.

"Your turn," I said.

"What?" Lia demanded.

"I said it's your turn—same exercise. Mom has just died and you are to speak at her funeral tomorrow. I want you to write out all the things you are going to miss about her. Write down what was good about having Gail as your mom."

Lia crossed her arms and Gail stopped writing. "I mean it," I said. "I'm tired of all the carping I'm hearing around here—get to it." They glared at each other a moment and then they both began to write. At first they seemed to struggle but soon the words began to flow. For ten minutes they both wrote about the things they loved and appreciated in each other under the fictional scenario that they were to present their words at a funeral for the other the next day.

When they finished I said, "Okay, Gail. It's time for the funeral. I'm the minister. I've just welcomed everyone and made my opening remarks. I've called you up to read the eulogy; let's hear it."

Softly, and without looking at Lia, Gail began to read. As she did, a lone tear began to stream down Lia's cheek, which she quickly wiped away.

When Gail finished I said, "What a wonderful celebration of life." I paused a moment to allow the energy in the room to absorb Gail's words, then said, "Lia, your turn." Lia glanced at her mom and then began to read. She spoke of the wonderful things her mother has been and done for her. Gail stared at the table and began to sniffle. Before Lia could finish her portion of the exercise they both erupted into a simultaneous shout of "I'm so sorry!" and rushed to hug each other.

Prior to this experience the two of them were focused on the things about each other they wished were different. Participating in this admittedly extreme but nonetheless poignant exercise, they were overcome with appreciation for the things they cherish about each other.

You alone have vision into that second pane of the Johari window. There are things about yourself that you see and others will never see. You have intimate knowledge about yourself and, as the old saying goes, with familiarity comes contempt. You probably have discounted your good qualities and focused on your flaws.

EXERCISE 1. Write your eulogy. Spend at least a half hour writing out the things that have been great about your life. Make note of your achievements and your contributions, however small. List the activities you have engaged in that have brought joy to others. If you need some help getting started, pick up a newspaper and read what others have said about the life of a loved one. Use phrases such as "devoted husband," "loving mother," "cherished sister," and so forth.

Whenever I perform a life celebration—my term for what many call a funeral—I ask the family to share stories that uniquely identify the person who has made their transition. Recently, I was honored to officiate at a life celebration for a man who attempted to build an airplane in his garage. When the man died, the plane he had worked on for nearly three decades was only about two-thirds complete. When I spoke to him a few weeks prior to his death, he lamented that he had never gotten around to finishing this project. He felt he had failed.

However, at his life celebration, his son told how his father never finished the plane because he spent most of his free time with him and his grandchildren. "My dad could have been shut away in the garage working on that plane," the son said, "and if he had, he would have finished it twenty years ago. But he chose to spend his time with me and with his grandchildren. My dad never missed a ballet recital, baseball game, or family picnic. His focus was on others and our lives will forever be better thanks to this. If he had finished it, it would have been an airplane; as it is, it's a monument to his life and his love for his family."

Ruthlessly edit your eulogy for any hint of regret or negativity. This is a *celebration* of a great person. And you are indeed a great person.

BONUS. Read your eulogy aloud while standing in front of a mirror every day for thirty days. You will be amazed at the shift that happens in your relationship with yourself if you do this.

EXERCISE 2. Write out those things that you consider your flaws. Yes, you heard correct. Put the words "My Flaws" on a piece of paper and start writing. Don't be surprised if you find, of all the exercises, that this one comes easiest; you are looking into that second pane of the Johari window, where you see things about yourself others do not.

Now, imagine you are writing a screenplay for a book or a treatment for a novel. Read the list again and consider these "flaws." Mentally assign them to the hero or heroine in a story and consider how these negative attributes are actually quirks that make this character unique.

Movies, books, and television shows are most enjoyable when we can relate to the characters. Characters who have only positive qualities, who are "too perfect," are difficult to relate with and we write them off as one-dimensional. You are not and never will be a one-dimensional person. You are multifaceted and the things about yourself that you consider the most challenging are oftentimes the things that best define you.

On your piece of paper, cross out "Flaws" and write "Quirks." What you consider to be your flaws often present expressed or latent strengths. Beside the list of ~~flaws~~ QUIRKS, write out possible corresponding positive attributes. If you wrote down that you are impatient, you may want to celebrate that you tend to complete tasks on time. If you noted that you are easily angered, you may discover that you are a passionate person. Henceforth, refuse to define your challenging qualities as flaws. They are not flaws; they are quirks. They are idiosyncrasies.

As you discover the strengths behind what you at first considered weaknesses, you can find ways to positively express these attributes and the things you felt were problematic about your personality will diminish.

4. NEVER ARGUE ABOUT REALITY.

Every life brings with it painful experiences. In the past you've done things you wish you could change. There are also things others have done that you wish had not happened.

When we get into a conflict with someone else over reality it is based on differing perspectives of what happened. When we get into a conflict with ourselves over reality it is most often about things that happened but which we feel *should not* have occurred.

To paraphrase best-selling author Byron Katie, there is one way to know if something should have happened and that is whether or not it happened. If it happened, it happened for a reason and there is a gift for you in the experience if you are willing to do some exploration. There are good things that can come from nearly any experience if we will delve deeply enough in our search for them.

On January 21, 1995, Tariq Khamisa was a 20-year-old college student in San Diego delivering pizzas to earn some extra money. While making a delivery, Tariq knocked at the door of the address listed on the pizza box only to discover that no one inside admitted to having ordered a pizza. Thinking the order was a prank, Tariq shrugged and walked briskly back to his car. As he approached his vehicle, he noticed a gang of rowdy teenagers approaching him. One of them, 14-year-old Tony Hicks, yearned to earn the respect of the older boys and was susceptible to their influence.

The boys began to taunt Tariq and demanded he give them the pizza. Tariq refused. They threatened Tariq and blocked the way to his car. "Give us the pizza, motherf——r!"

Tariq was composed and steadfast. "No," he said.

"Shoot 'im!" said one. "Kill the bastard!" The voice was that of one of the senior gang members; he looked at young Tony Hicks as he spoke. "Shoot him!"

In that moment, Hicks's desire to be accepted by the other boys surpassed his grandfather's stern teaching about right and wrong. Hicks pulled out a gun and fired. Tariq fell dead.

Tariq's father, Azim, was crushed by grief. As realities go, this was particularly excruciating. Rather than being consumed and debilitated by his loss, however, Azim Khamisa chose to use his son's tragic death as a platform to help others. He reached out to Plez Felix, Tony Hicks's grandfather and legal guardian, and the two began a dialogue. They discussed how each of them had lost a child; Khamisa's son was dead and Felix's grandson was facing a murder charge. Even though Hicks was only 14, the state of California sought to try him as an adult. "From the onset, I saw victims on both ends of the gun," Azim said. In their discussions, Khamisa and Felix decided to work together to help stop such senseless violence.

They established the Tariq Khamisa Foundation (www.tkf.org) and the two now speak to groups of parents and young people to "help kids stop killing kids." Khamisa says, "In my faith, on the fortieth day after a death you are encouraged to channel your grief into good, compassionate deeds, deeds which provide high-octane fuel for the soul's forward journey. Forty days is not a long time to grieve for a child, but one of my motivations for starting the Tariq Khamisa Foundation was to create spiritual currency for my son, as well as to give myself a sense of purpose."

Tony Hicks will be eligible for parole in 2017. Azim Khamisa is an advocate for his release and has offered Tony a job when he is free.

You may have experienced something every bit as painful as what Azim Khamisa lived through. Do you wish it had never happened? Of course. But it did happen. The question becomes, "What you are going to do to move past the experience?" How can you find high-octane fuel for your soul's forward journey?

Whatever it was, accept that it happened and move forward

without feeling it should not have occurred. Don't argue about reality. It happened—that's reality.

EXERCISE 1. Make a list of the events in your life that you wish
you could change or do over.

EXERCISE 2. For each of those events you've listed, write down
the answers to the following questions.

- How am I a better person for having survived this experience?
- What have I learned from going through this that has helped
  me?
- How can I share what I have learned to help others?
- How can I take what has happened to me and let it serve as
  the high-octane soul fuel I need to prevent this from happening to others?

5. EMBRACE FORGIVENESS AND POSITIVE INTENT.

It has been theorized that human beings cannot do anything they
know to be wrong. That's a sweeping statement and seems contrary to the evidence of what people do, but if
you think about it, there is some truth in this.

> All forgiveness
> is, ultimately,
> self-forgiveness.
> —MICHAEL BECKWITH

If a child strikes another child, the parent
may often rush over and ask the offending
child, "Why did you do that?" The child will
typically have an answer. It may be "Because
she took my toy" or "Because he called me a name." Most children are taught from an early age that hitting anyone is wrong
and yet they still may hit from time to time. If they know that
this is wrong, why do they do it? They do what they know to be
wrong because they have a *reason* for doing it. They have a justi-

fication for their action. The act is no longer "wrong"; it seems warranted given the circumstances.

Could there have been a better way to handle the situation? Of course. But in that moment the child experienced dissatisfaction and, rather than taking time to discover what would relieve the dissatisfaction without hitting, did something that he or she had been told was wrong.

We might say, "The child was wrong not to have taken the time to weigh the options and make a better choice." Not necessarily. First of all, we are talking about a *child.* Their emotional resources are limited. Remember, both life and relationships are about growth and at a young age the child simply hasn't had enough relational schooling to have a wealth of tools to handle most situations.

Second, if you were to ask the child, "Why didn't you take the time to consider what you might do rather than hitting?" the child would have an answer: "Because he was hurting my doll," or "Because I've tried everything to get him to stop calling me names; I'm tired of it!"

Whenever we do something we know to be wrong, we have a reason for our behavior. It is no longer wrong; it is justified. This may seem like nothing more than rationalizing the behavior but in the person's mind is the thought, "This rule that this is wrong no longer applies. Desperate times call for desperate measures."

You have done things you know to be wrong. But in that moment your resources for dealing with the issue were not sufficient to allow you to find a way to get your needs met without breaking the rules. You may have been tired, frustrated, angry, hungry, or simply in a new and uncomfortable situation. In that moment, you did what was "wrong" but you had a reason for doing it. Therefore, your actions were not wrong; they were justifiable.

There is a joke about a woman who was cut off in traffic by someone. The woman, having had a tough day already, became enraged and drove up alongside the offending driver. Honking her horn to get the driver's attention, she rolled down her window and began to let loose a cascade of insults and expletives. To punctuate her discourse, she gave the other driver the "We're Number 1" sign with the wrong finger.

Rolling her window back up, she saw in the mirror the lights of an approaching police car. "Good," she thought. "The cops saw this jerk cut me off and are going to arrest him." Instead, the officer pulled in behind the woman and waved *her* to the side of the road. Shocked, the woman did as she was instructed.

"Get out of the car with your hands up!" the cop's voice boomed through the loudspeaker. Now frightened, the woman stepped tentatively out onto the street.

"Facedown on the ground!" the officer ordered.

The woman dropped slowly to her knees and then lay prostrate on the ground. She felt cold handcuffs being clicked onto her wrists. She was dragged off and placed into the back of the squad car. As the officer drove her away, she saw a tow truck carrying away her car to be impounded.

For several hours she sat in a holding cell without being told the offense she was being charged with or what her fate might be. Finally an officer opened the cell door and said flatly, "You're free to go."

As the officer escorted her out, the woman became agitated. She spun around and asked, "Why was I arrested? What the hell is going on here!?"

The police officer explained, "The arresting officer saw how you treated the other driver and then saw the 'What Would Jesus Do?' and 'Visualize World Peace' bumper stickers on your vehicle. Based on the contrast between your actions and the bumper stickers, the officer figured the car *must* have been stolen."

Faced with the traffic situation, the woman had justified her behavior as not being wrong even though it ran contrary to her deeply held convictions.

You, too, have done things you knew to be wrong but which were not wrong to you in the moment you did them. Carrying guilt for these past actions removes the context in which you did them and simply writes you off as wrong. You have felt guilt, remorse, and regret for things you have done and yet, given the circumstances and your level of spiritual growth as well as the emotional resources at the time, you only did what you were capable of doing.

It is time to let go of the resentments you hold against yourself. It is time for you to forgive youself. Forgiving others is difficult; forgiving ourselves can be nearly impossible because we often hold ourselves to standards that are unrealistically rigorous.

Just as you have worked to forgive others, now do the same for yourself.

EXERCISE 1. Sit quietly, eyes closed, and begin to breathe deeply. Imagine you are seated front row center in a large, opulent theater. You are alone in this large theater and feel a sense of detachment, a sense of bliss. Notice the large drapes that decorate the stage before you. The house lights begin to dim and are replaced by a lone spotlight casting a large circle of light on the center of the curtains.

Stare at the circle of light and take several more deep breaths. Then, when you feel ready, see *yourself* stepping forward into the bright light. Visualize yourself holding a small blank chalkboard. Take another deep breath and, in the quiet of your mind, say,

> [YOUR NAME], I now release all resentment I have held against you. I welcome you into the bright light of a new day and see you with a clean slate. I celebrate the things you have taught me and give thanks for the gift you are in my life.

Then begin to applaud for yourself and watch your self take this in. Watch as the you standing on the stage possibly begins to weep for having been forgiven for what you have done. Spend some time looking into your own eyes as you appreciate and celebrate yourself. Then, as before, invite yourself to come toward you.

However, as this newly forgiven you comes toward you, rather than having this self sit down at your side as others you have forgiven did; imagine standing up and the two of you melding back together into a single, newly forgiven version of yourself.

This may take several attempts for you to feel completely absolved. Invest the time and then journal about the experience and how it feels to be forgiven.

EXERCISE 2. If you are having trouble with this exercise, remember that we all do what we do with a positive intention. Journal answers to these questions:

- What was my underlying intent for what I did?
- What need was I attempting to have met?
- Given what I now know, how might I act differently in the future?

Now, repeat the forgiveness exercise. Breathe and you will begin to feel as the woman in the joke felt after she was released from jail—it was just a misunderstanding.

6. BECOME COMPLAINT FREE.

The primary relationship we all have is with ourselves. Other relationships are an outward demonstration of this inner, primary relationship. We want to have healthy, empowering, and satisfying relationships with others and to do this we must first have that type of relationship with ourselves.

Complaining designates you as a victim of your circumstances. You cannot be an empowered, fully functioning person if you are a victim.

EXERCISE 1. Visit our website, www.AComplaintFreeWorld.org, and get one of our purple bracelets. Or put a rubber band on your wrist. Every time you catch yourself complaining, switch the bracelet to the other wrist. With every movement of the bracelet you are now back at day one. The goal is to make being Complaint Free habitual and psychologists believe it takes 21 days for an activity to become a habit. It may take you many months to go 21 consecutive days without complaining but in the process you will transform your inner self.

The mind is a manufacturer; it produces thoughts. The mouth is a customer; it buys what is produced and speaks the thoughts aloud. When the customer stops buying what the manufacturer is producing, the manufacturer retools. Most people have a steady stream of negative thoughts running through their minds that then spew forth as complaints. When you stop complaining, you will find that your mental hard drive reformats and you become a happier person.

> The mind is a manufacturer; it produces thoughts.
>
> The mouth is a customer that buys what is produced, speaking the thoughts aloud.
>
> When the customer stops buying what the manufacturer is producing, the manufacturer will retool.

EXERCISE 2. Make a list of what you typically complain about. Then ask yourself if the underlying motivation behind your gripe is to:

- <u>G</u>et Attention
- <u>R</u>emove yourself from responsibility
- <u>I</u>nspire envy or brag
- Have <u>P</u>ower over someone
- <u>E</u>xcuse your poor performance

EXERCISE 3. Write out alternative things you can do to get these needs met. Plumb the depths of your limitless mind to find ways to achieve things you once thought impossible. What you give, you will receive.

- If your desire is to get attention, recognize someone else. Give that person attention and see that the bond, not recognition for yourself, is actually what you were searching for.
- Rather than removing yourself from responsibility, ask how, in whatever small way, you *are* able to respond and improve a situation.
- If you feel an urge to brag, recognize that it is coming from being too self-focused. How might you focus on and serve others and feel better about yourself in the process?
- If you desire to have power over another, it comes from a feeling of powerlessness in yourself. How can you feel powerful by considering, embracing, and acting on your options?

Understanding your internal motivation for complaining and finding alternatives to being a victim empowers you. Becoming Complaint Free changes your mind-set and lets you see the beauty within and around you.

◈

All relationships are, ultimately, with ourselves. Your internal relationship plays out in each of your external relationships. Beginning to develop a healthy and loving association with the one person you can never be separate from transmutes all of your relationships. When you positively transform your relationships with yourself others will treat you better. By transforming your relationship with yourself you change the context of your relationships with others from an opportunity to project your unhealed stuff onto them to an opportunity for mutual fun and growth. Their relationship with you will begin to shift as well as they sense this, and they will begin to respond in more collaborative and supportive ways.

Genuine, authentic relationships must begin with discovering, forgiving, and celebrating your genuine, authentic self. If you are dedicated to having healthy, happy, and supportive relationships, they all begin within.

Opening Up

Trying to improve your relationships with others without healing your relationship with yourself is futile and any results will be short-lived.

This chapter offers exercises that will help you reform the most important and lasting relationship you will ever have. Begin now to invest a half hour each day into building a solid foundation for all of your relationships by transforming your relationship with yourself.

CHAPTER 7

It's Not Personal; It's Personal

Everything that irritates us about others can lead us to an understanding of ourselves.

—CARL JUNG

We have seen that complaining does not improve relationships. Rather, complaining tends to compound and perpetuate relationship challenges. But there is another, very compelling reason not to complain in relationships.

An article in the American Psychological Association's *Journal of Personality and Social Psychology* reports that when you complain, the listener actually ascribes the negative traits you are griping about back to you. In their findings, titled "Spontaneous Trait Transference: Communicators Take on the Qualities They Describe in Others," the authors write, "Politicians who allege corruption by their opponents may themselves be perceived as dishonest and gossips who describe others' infidelities may themselves be viewed as immoral."

> · When you complain about someone else, people hearing you complain assign those negative traits to you.

You may be complaining to or about someone to get an interpersonal need met. You may desire attention.

You may be complaining to brag that you are superior to someone. Or you may be complaining to excuse your poor performance in a relationship. But the person hearing you gripe subconsciously concludes that *you* have the very same negative characteristics.

It all comes back to you.

Why is this? Why would someone hearing you complain about another person think that you have the traits you are complaining about? The reason is that we see in others those attributes that we do not know we possess. The things that bother us about someone tend to be things about ourselves that reside in the third pane of the Johari window—the part of ourselves we do not see. Complaining is our subconscious way of bringing these issues up so we can work on them.

I recently had a personal experience of this. I was sitting in my office waiting for some late arrivers for a meeting. As I waited, I found anxious and critical thoughts running through my mind, including, "Where the heck are they? This is disrespectful of my time and the time of others." Catching myself in this negativity, I pulled out my calendar and, while I waited, I checked the meetings I had been involved in over the previous week. If someone was coming to see me—that is, if I was already in my office—I was typically on time. However, in seven out of nine meetings that I had *away* from my office, I ran late. I was tardy for meetings with others more than 70 percent of the time. No wonder I was upset with people doing likewise. My dissatisfaction with their behavior was a call for me to review my own performance, which I did. I'm more punctual now and more tolerant of those who are not.

There is something inside us that knows that the things we find most distasteful in others are often unresolved issues or attributes of ourselves. This is why others ascribe the content of our complaints back onto us. Relationships help us grow; growth is discovering the things about ourselves that need to heal and change. Growth can only come through change and areas for growth are many times brought to the surface via conflicts with other people. When you feel like complaining about another person, first seek to discover if you share the same behavior.

> Everybody wants things to get better but nobody wants things to change.
>
> —PAT PARELLI

You may discover that you do indeed have the same behavior; if so, realizing it in this manner provides an opportunity for you to change and grow. However, what you may discover is that you do not share the behavior but rather have unhealed energy *about* this behavior.

Recently a woman came to me for counseling. She told me that for nearly two years she had an ongoing challenge with a coworker. The coworker often came to work late, leaving this woman to handle more than her share of tasks or let the tasks remain undone. The coworker would leave early and/or spend part of the workday pursuing personal matters, again causing this woman to feel she needed to do not only her work but the coworker's as well.

"She's irresponsible!" the woman angrily said to me, and she went on to describe in great detail how victimized she felt by the coworker's behavior and how powerless she felt to correct the situation.

"In what ways might you also be irresponsible?" I asked.

The woman thought a moment and then began to share with me how tremendously responsible she was in both her work and her family life. As she spoke, her tone was calm and matter-of-fact. She did not sound resentful or as if she were trying to convince me and herself that she was indeed a person who honors her commitments. She was simply a responsible person.

"Okay," I said. "Who else in your life has been irresponsible?"

"*My father!*" she blurted out. Her tone and her speed in answering indicated there was some unhealed energy around her relationship with him. "There were six of us kids," she said, "and he never did anything to help my mom around the house. He was off doing God knows what. She took care of us *and* worked full-time to support us. Then he would recklessly spend our rent money on whatever caught his fancy. I remember once our rent was past due and my mother managed to scrape together just enough to get it current. Well, he found the money and bought a boat! Can you believe it? His wife and six children were about to be tossed out onto the street and he used our only money to buy a damn boat!"

"How did this make you feel?" I asked.

"Helpless . . . powerless," she said, her hands shaking with rage at the memory of her father's irresponsibility and her inability as a small child to get him to be accountable for his family's needs.

"So you have a real problem with your coworker being irresponsible. Her behavior has been upsetting you for a long time, right?"

"Yes," she said.

"And you feel powerless to get her to change, right?"

"Yes."

"It sounds to me like this is not about your issue with the woman at work; it's about some unhealed issues with your father," I said. "It makes sense that you would have felt powerless over your father's behavior; you were just a little girl when he squandered the rent. But as a fully grown, accomplished professional, there are things you can do to improve the situation at work, right?"

She thought for a moment and then agreed.

"Do some journaling about your feelings about your father," I said. "Perhaps imagine you're talking to the little girl that was you back then. Be with her in her pain and frustration; let her know it's legitimate to feel as she does considering your father's actions. Or in your journaling you might mentally go back as the strong adult you are now and intervene. Have a bold conversation with your father as he was back then and let him know that his behavior will not be tolerated."

This woman felt like a helpless child at work when faced with her coworker's behavior. Others at her job simply let the coworker fail and did not attempt to cover for her. But this woman felt a burning need to step in and do what the coworker was not willing to do. And she felt powerless to ask or insist that the woman be responsible. This was a carry-over from her childhood. Her growth opportunity was not in realizing that irresponsibility was a behavior she possessed; rather, it was to discover that she carried negative energy and associations about her father. The growth area was in her relationship with her father, a relationship that still existed in her mind (as do all relationships) even though her father had passed away decades before.

As we've said, people complain to get attention, remove themselves from responsibility, inspire envy, have power over others, and excuse their poor performance. These are the reasons *why* people complain. But *what* do people tend to complain about? What are the common things in relationships about which people are dissatisfied and which lead them to complain? Dr. J. K. Alberts discovered five broad dissatisfaction categories:

Dissatisfaction	Example
1. Behavior (about another's actions or lack thereof)	*"You left your socks on the floor again!"*
2. Personal characteristics (about another's personalities or beliefs)	*"You're a loudmouth; you talk nonstop and never listen to other people!"*
3. Performance (about how actions are performed)	*"You're not planting that tree correctly; you should dig the hole deeper!"*
4. Complaining (about another's complaint behavior)	*"You are always griping at me!"*
5. Personal appearance	*"Your hair is a mess; did you even bother to run a comb through it this morning?"*

Of the dissatisfaction characteristics listed above, Alberts discovered that *behavioral complaints accounted for fully 72 percent of all complaints in relationships.* Think about that. In relationships, nearly three-fourths of all the complaints uttered are about what the other person does or does not do. In fact, people tend to complain about another person's behavior nearly five times more often than the next most frequently cited reason (personal characteristics, 17 percent) and three times more than all the others combined!

But there is more to a complaint than the reason it is presented. Beyond the motivation of the complainer there is the way it is *received* by the other person. And here is the interesting part: even though an overwhelming majority of complaints are about a person's behavior, people hearing complaints directed toward them tend to hear these complaints as personal attacks. Recipients of behavioral complaints internalize these comments as disparaging remarks about themselves personally.

Alberts conducted a study of 52 couples who were asked to both express complaints to and receive complaints from their partners. Each person was then interviewed as to the nature of the complaints.

> Studies have found that people tend to hear complaints about their behavior as personal attacks.

People in the study remembered giving more behavioral complaints than personal characteristic complaints. When asked, they estimated that they complained about 20 percent more often about the other person's behavior as opposed to complaints about the other person's personal characteristics. They estimated that the majority of the complaints they gave were behavioral rather than personal.

However, when asked about the complaints they received, the participants estimated that they received personal complaints approximately 30 percent more often than they received behavioral complaints. They felt the complaints they received were personal more than behavioral.

But the experimenters carefully monitored the quality and quantity of the complaints and found there was no significant difference between complaint types given. In other words, in this study the complaints about the other person's behavior were about 50 percent of the total and the remaining 50 percent were about them personally. The complaints were equally about a person's behavior and about their personal characteristics. But the people giving the complaints thought they were talking more often about the other's behavior, whereas the people receiving the complaints heard the complaints as predominantly personal.

Both partners significantly overestimated the number of personal complaints they received. And they underestimated the number of personal complaints they delivered. They thought their partners were criticizing them personally, whereas the partners felt they were simply pointing out aspects of the other person's behavior for possible improvement.

This clearly explains the challenges in most relationships. You think you're giving neutral feedback to someone. But you hear another person's feedback as him or her personally maligning you. And, the other person feels the exact same way. Talk about "when worlds collide!"

This study is important to remember whenever we deliver or receive comments. When someone shares feedback with us, the comments are most often about our behavior but we will tend to take them personally. When we share feedback with others, even if our comments are about their behavior, they will tend to take our comments personally.

Harking back to our discussion of the "Dissatisfaction ➞ Complaint" loop, this explains why complaints are so often responded to with countercomplaints. You may express dissatisfaction with another person's behavior. Your comment is about something the other person has or has not done; it is *not* a personal attack. However, the comment is interpreted as a personal attack and responded to by counterattack. One of the most consistent findings of studies about complaining in relationships is that dissatisfied couples are more likely to cross-complain—they respond to a complaint with a complaint. And this explains why. Comments delivered as behavioral observations are received and responded to as personal attacks.

So when someone complains to you, resist the knee-jerk reaction to take it personally. What that person says is far more likely to be a comment about a behavior of yours. Behaviors are changeable. They are things about which we often are not aware but which may bother the other person. And if we are truly committed to creating satisfying relationships, behaviors are something we may consider dropping or changing to maintain harmony.

When you make a comment to another person, make it clear that your statement is not a judgment of his or her value. For example: "I want you to know that I think you are terrific. So please know that this isn't personal. It's just that when you leave the toilet seat up and I go to the bathroom in the middle of the night, I fall into the bowl. Thank you for lifting the lid when you go to the bathroom; that's very considerate. Would you please put the seat down when you are finished?"

You sometimes need to overemphasize that a comment is about a person's behavior so that he or she will not take it personally. Otherwise the person may become defensive and be less likely to comply with your request.

If you react strongly to a comment about a behavior, it is typically because it is something about which you are not consciously aware. However, deep inside, you know the behavior exists. Your strong reaction is a good indicator that you need to consider the other person's comment and discover what about it brings up your intense energy.

For example, if a person at work tends to take things from your desk and not return them, you may get perturbed. You have a right to have your things returned to you. You ask the person to either return your things to you or stop borrowing them. This is a request for a change of behavior; it's not personal. This is a neutral request spoken directly and only to the person responsible. This is healthy communication. This is affirming your rights. This is taking responsibility for getting your needs met.

> Our strong reaction is a good indicator that we need to consider the other person's comment and discover what about it brings up our intense energy.

However, your coworker may hear your request as a personal assault: "Are you calling me a thief?" If this happens, something inside this person has been touched. Perhaps as a child his or her parents withheld material items as punishment. Perhaps as a teenager the person was wrongly arrested for stealing and is hypersensitive to any suggestion he or she would take something belonging to somebody else. Regardless of the reason, your request was aimed at a change in behavior; it was not a personal attack. Your coworker, however, took it personally.

When someone offers a request for a change in behavior it is tempting for us to take the comment personally. It is important to understand that the comment *is* personal—personal to the other person. The request is coming from that person's unique perspective on reality, his or her personal world. Even if the comment is a personal attack directed at you, it is coming from the other person's unique history of relationships and relationship issues. It is personal—to them; not to you. It is *their* stuff.

We do ourselves a disservice and diminish harmony in our relationships when we take others' comments personally. These remarks are coming from the other people's perspective, which is a simmering stew filled with stories they have told themselves about you, others, and themselves. They are looking at the relationship and/or the situation in the context of the pictures they have hung in their mind based on their past experiences.

Is it personal? Yes.

Is it about you? No.

In other words, it's personal; it's not personal.

Having this understanding can be freeing. "Their reaction is not about me, it's about them" can help wipe clean a lot of the negative energy when others complain. However, it should not be an excuse to resist hearing things about ourselves that we genuinely need to know as part of our life's growth experience. So how do we know when a comment or complaint is a person projecting his or her stuff onto us and when it is truly something for us to consider?

Look for patterns in the comments you receive. When you begin to hear or experience similar comments from several people, you should begin to review if it is indeed your issue to deal with. Consider processing about the experience with someone and ask for honest feedback to help see yourself more clearly.

If you do discover that there is something for you to work on, remember that what you are working on is a *behavior*. It's not a commentary about you as a person. It is not that you are bad or that you are not of value. You are of infinite value simply because you are alive. But as we discussed, we all have things that need to be taken into the light so they can be healed and released. Use the suggestions in the previous chapter to do some work around the issue and then ask a neutral person you trust for feedback as to how you are doing.

As we've discussed, everyone has had challenging experiences that have left unhealed issues. We are born unique individuals with great gifts and strengths. When we are children, however, sometimes these strengths and gifts are not celebrated; they may even be criticized or squelched. A child may be raised in a home with a parent prone to rage and therefore does everything possible to go unnoticed, potentially developing a personality pattern that is withdrawn, indirect, and nonassertive. The underlying message is, "If you don't see me, you can't hurt me."

By contrast, a child may be raised in a home where the parents do not provide loving attention, a family where there is little or no direct connection, a home where the television blares day and night to act as a buffer to the occasional awkwardness of human relationships. This person may grow up to be loud, boisterous, and overly assertive. He or she may be seen as overbearing. The underlying message of his or her personality is, "I'm here! I'm alive! Notice me!"

Our behaviors are often the evidence of emotional scar tissue from our childhood. Growing through life means discovering these old wounds and doing some work around them. Our parents are human, just as we are. They had their own challenges. As parents, we do our best, but often our emotional scars get passed along to our children.

A common emotional scar carried by many people is the belief that their parents acted in negative ways toward them because they somehow *deserved* such treatment. They take their parents' behavior personally. Whether or not the parents made any comments to this effect, they internalize their parents' behavior as a negative comment about their worth. Rather than understanding it as the parents' unhealed issues playing out in the home, they take the parents' behaviors as indicators that they were the cause of the problem. "If only I'd been different, they would have treated me differently," they think.

> Behaviors are often the evidence of emotional scar tissue from childhood.

Growth comes in understanding that your parents' behavior was an outer expression of *their* issues, not yours. Your parents' behavior was an indicator of where your parents were in their growth at the time; you happened to be an unwitting character in an act of the play that is their life. In later scenes your parents may have changed, or they may not. Either way, their behavior was their issue; it was not a disparagement of your value.

Issues that come up in relationships may seem challenging, enormous, even terrible, but they present themselves to be healed. And they are healed through love. The great German poet Ranier Maria Rilke declared, "Everything terrible is something that needs our love." Our challenges with ourselves can be healed by love. Our challenges with how our mother and father parented us can be healed through love. Our challenges with others with whom we share relationships can be healed through love.

> Relationships are a microcosm of the great macrocosm that is our lives.

We need to remember why we are here. We are here to have fun and to grow—that's what life is all about. And relationships are a microcosm of the great macrocosm that is our lives. They are little drops in the ocean of our existence. They provide us with fun and they provide us with growth.

A man I know was at a crossroads in his life. He was in a job he dearly loved. His job provided him with inspiring challenges that allowed him to grow and to creatively apply his skills. He was well compensated for his work and he had the respect and admiration of others in his field.

But there was one issue at work he could not seem to overcome. The people with whom he worked seemed hopelessly incompetent. They did not perform tasks to his standard nor in the time frame he felt was reasonable. They were not friendly to him; they seemed to whisper conspiratorially behind his back. And yet, he noticed, they got along well with one another.

For months he worked hard and continued to achieve outer success but his dissatisfaction with his staff continued. On the verge of leaving his beloved position, he instead took an extended vacation to weigh his options.

"Should I quit?" he wondered one night as he lay in bed.

"Maybe I should just fire everyone and hire an all-new staff," he thought as he strolled barefoot along the beach.

"Maybe I should bring in a consultant," he considered while lying in a hammock beneath the stars. "Someone to whip these folks into shape."

He told me that for the first several days of his vacation his mind was consumed with the ineptitude of this team and his overwhelming desire to replace them or quit. He could not decide which to do.

"What did you finally settle on?" I asked him.

"That's the funny thing," he said. "For days I considered my options and thought of new things I might consider, but nothing seemed to be the right answer. Over time I just forgot about it all and had fun with my family.

"But here's the interesting part," he said, leaning in close. "When I got back, I found that all the work had been done. And, more than that, everyone was treating me with a newfound appreciation and respect."

"What changed while you were away?" I asked.

"I did," he said. "I unwound and had fun. I remembered the important things in life. I was no longer consumed with petty things at work. When I left I was wound up tight as a spring, and when I came back I was relaxed. I felt gentle with myself and I acted gently toward them. They responded to the new me and things are great."

That is true of all relationships. When we change, they change. When we take responsibility for creating our relationships, we give ourselves the power to improve them. That is the power we have. We can create strife-ridden or Complaint Free relationships; the choice is ours. We can improve our relationships. If we take responsibility for our relationships, we can transform them.

Albert Einstein summed it up well: "A human being is part of a whole, called by us the Universe, a part limited in time and space. He experiences himself, his thoughts and feelings, as something separated from the rest—a kind of optical delusion of his consciousness. This delusion is a kind of prison for us, restricting us to our personal desires and to affection for a few persons nearest us. Our task must be to free ourselves from this prison by widening our circles of compassion to embrace all living creatures and the whole of nature in its beauty."

Opening Up

1. When someone makes a comment and you are tempted to take it personally, remember that it *is* personal—to the other person. It is not about you. Take a moment to consider what may be happening in the other person's life either currently or in the past to cause him or her to speak to you this way. Journal about what might be the real cause and release any back story your ego mind has that makes this somehow about you. It is not.

2. When you receive complaints from different people notice any patterns that emerge. Rather than disregarding these comments, take what you hear as valuable feedback and journal as to what you might do to change your behavior if you feel that doing so would be beneficial.

3. Make a list of your strengths. Everyone has them. What are you uniquely good at? What talents and skills do you possess? When criticism comes your way, mentally run through this list and remember that you are a multifaceted person who has many great qualities. Give thanks for your strengths and explore your growth areas as just the ongoing finishing touches of life.

4. When you have something to share with someone else about his or her behavior, consider how you might make it clear that your comments are not personal. Write down what you might say. Tell the person what you perceive to be his or her good qualities and express your gratitude for the things you admire. Let the person know that your comments are not intended personally and then explain specifically what you would like his or her *behavior* to be. *Don't talk about what the person has done in the past; say what you would like him or her to do in the future.*

5. Know your worth. If someone complains to you, refuse to take that comment as an estimate of your worth. Affirm, "I am of inestimable value."

Conclusion

*The fault, dear Brutus, lies not in our stars, but
in ourselves.*

—WILLIAM SHAKESPEARE, *JULIUS CAESAR*

Esteemed Indian philosopher and spiritualist Jiddu Krishnamurti wrote, "There is no end to relationship. There may be the end of a particular relationship, but relationship can never end; to be is to be related."

Relationships are and always will be a part of your life.

Your relationships can be your greatest problem and your relationships can be your greatest blessing. Sometimes they will be both simultaneously.

A relationship may last from conception until death or it may grace your life for mere seconds. Regardless of a relationship's tenure, in every moment *all* relationships are in transition. Relationships are always shifting and changing because we are always and forever shifting, changing, and growing.

The fact that we and our relationships are in flux does not mean we are unable to repair and

> There is no end
> to relationship.
> There may be the
> end of a particular
> relationship, but
> relationship can
> never end; to be
> is to be related.
>
> —JIDDU KRISHNAMURTI

improve them; quite the opposite. The very fact that relationships *are* characterized by transition means that we can alter their course. They have a direction that is created in large measure by who we are and what we tell ourselves about the other person.

To positively transform our relationships we must embrace that we are already directing our relationships. Our opportunity is to awaken to this fact and begin to guide the course of our relationships with intention. To find fulfillment where once there may have been frustration. To find harmony where there was once discord. This is possible only when we make the decision to be proactive in our relationships rather than reactive, to seize the reins and move the relationship in the direction of our choosing.

My family and I have four beautiful horses. Occasionally we will invite a friend to ride with us and Gail, Lia, and I will load up our horses along with our "spare" horse, Dove. Prior to our acquiring Dove, she was a kids' riding camp horse. She's a perfect mount for guests because most people can ride her regardless of their level of equestrian expertise.

We were once riding along a narrow trail, with Gail in the lead, Lia in second place, followed by our friend aboard Dove, and I and my horse bringing up the rear. I noticed our friend was having some challenges. Dove kept leaving the trail and walking into the woods on the right side of the slender trail. When she did, her rider pulled the reins and Dove returned to the path.

"What's the matter?" I asked.

"Dove won't stay on the trail," our friend said with obvious frustration. "She keeps veering off to the right."

"That's because you're telling her to veer to the right," I said.

"No, I'm not," she said.

I could see that our friend was, in fact, telling Dove to divert from the trail but she had no awareness she was doing it. She truly thought she was asking Dove to go straight. She blamed Dove for their unexpected right turns and for their getting scratched by the low-hanging branches that border the trail.

"Yes," I said, "you are. You keep twisting your upper body to the right when you talk over your shoulder to me. When you do, Dove senses your movement and assumes you want her to turn in that direction. She's just responding to you. When you talk to me, try keeping your body aimed forward and just turning your head. If you turn your body, Dove is going to move in that direction."

At first it wasn't easy for her to remember but after a while our friend got into the habit of keeping her body facing up the trail and only turning her head to chat. Dove never strayed for the remainder of our ride. Having understood that she was the deciding factor as to whether or not Dove stayed on course, the woman faced the direction she wanted and Dove obediently responded.

If she and Dove had been standing still, it would have made little difference which way her body pointed. If they were not moving, they could not have gone off course. And if they were already off course but had stopped, she could not have gotten them back on the trail regardless of what she did. It was the fact that they were moving that allowed her to define the direction they walked in.

Your relationships are always moving, always progressing, and as a result, you can direct their course. Forget how many times you have gone off the trail previously. You did so because you did not know you were able to choose your path. You had dropped the reins. You had twisted your body in one direction or another and the relationship had responded. Now take the reins in your hands and direct the relationship up the trail of your choosing.

Remember, you are *already* directing the course of your relationships. You are deciding whether a relationship moves along a gentle path or gets diverted into the woods. The most important thing you can do is to understand that your relationships are *your* relationships. When you place the progression of a relationship into the hands of someone else, you remove your hands from the reins.

We shape our relationships with the thoughts that we hold and the resulting actions we take. A relationship is like a field. It can be a beautiful meadow in which we sow seeds of exploration and growth or it can be a battlefield scorched with pain and suffering. You decide the course of your relationships. You—not God, not the other person, not your horoscope, not karma, not the situation, not your age, not your race, not your upbringing, not how much money you have—decide where your relationships proceed.

Relationships provide us with many and varied expressions of fun and they provide us with opportunities to expand our love and compassion for ourselves and for others. All relationships are unique.

There are some people with whom we resonate immediately and there are others with whom we will simply never click. The type of relationship you have with one person as compared to the relationship you have with another does not make one person good and the other person bad; nor does this cast judgment upon our own value. Each soul's journey is unique and there are people who share and support your path and others who are not intended to do so.

There are people you resonate with from the moment you meet them. They fit with you like a custom-made suit with a perfectly matched tie. Both of you feel a kinship from the moment you meet. I call this a top-tier relationship.

Your connection with such people may have ups and downs but the relationship remains strong and steady as long as the relationship lasts. If you apply the principles we have outlined in this book, you will find yourself able to smooth out any rough spots you encounter with these special people.

There are others who simply do not seem to fit with you. Applying the lessons we have covered will give you the skills to lessen the challenges and find joy in these relationships as well. However, you will not be able to transform every relationship into a top-tier relationship. Nor should you want to. If all relationships were equally satisfying, you would not know the magnificence of a relationship that seems to transcend time and territory. These relationships are rare as diamonds. To try to force a relationship to be a top-tier relationship is futile and counterproductive.

In nearly every relationship there are times of discomfort. This is true not only in our relationships with others but also in our relationship with ourselves. There are times when we feel awkward, uncomfortable, anxious, and lost. In Western culture, there is a belief that there is something wrong with these moments of discomfort, yet nothing could be further from the truth.

Remember that relationships exist to provide growth. It is through times of discomfort that we discover areas we might address so we can grow. Again to compare a relationship to a field, sometimes weeds pop up regardless of the diligent and loving care you give the field. It is during these times of discord that you discover the next step along your personal evolution. You get to see the weeds so you can remove them before they overtake your crop. Challenging times afford glimpses into that third pane of your Johari window. The challenging times are signals. They are a call for new growth. They are not pinpointing flaws in the relationship. They are an indication that the relationship is ready to grow and move forward.

> There is a belief that times of pain and dissatisfaction are to be avoided at all cost. If we do this, we do so at our own peril, for it is during these times that we grow.

Some believe that times of pain and dissatisfaction are to be avoided at all cost. If we avoid them, we do so at our own peril, for it is during these times that we grow. They are a natural part of our soul's progression. To deny them is to deny growth. And yet the pharmaceutical industry, capitalizing on this very normal experience of discomfort and dissatisfaction, has sought to numb us to the experience with a bevy of antidepressant and anti-anxiety medications.

There are some people who benefit greatly from such medications and who truly need them to function. These drugs have helped a great many. And I'm not suggesting you or anyone else stop taking these medications suddenly; research has found that doing so can have disastrous results. However, millions of people who are on these drugs have bought into the illusion that life must always feel comfortable and be without challenges.

Being without problems, struggles, and discomfort is not life; that's death.

Going to a party presents a telling analogy for life. Most people feel a level of discomfort when they arrive at a party. After being at the party for some time there is a settling-in that occurs, and once this happens most people find themselves at ease. However, if you take those very same people to another party, en route they will probably begin to feel their angst returning. When they arrive at the second party, the discomfort returns for a while until they settle in and once again begin to feel more comfortable.

Relationships are like going from party to party. What's different from one party to the next? The people are different, so we have to figure out how to fit in with them. In relationships, we and the other person are always changing, so there is a *constant* state of settling in. This is normal and ongoing.

Many people drink alcohol to expedite the settling-in process when they arrive at a party. Why? Because the alcohol changes them. Alcohol consumption does not change the people around them. It changes the person doing the drinking, and as that person changes, the party seems to become more comfortable, more hospitable, and more enjoyable. It is when the person changes that the party changes for him or her.

Relationships are the same. As we change, the relationship must—not *may*, *must*—change as well. We transform relationships by transforming ourselves.

You may tell anyone who will listen that your relationship with this or that person is the most important thing in your life. You may say that you want the relationship to improve. You may spend thousands of dollars on books like this one, seminars, counseling, and other helpful avenues. But until you are willing to change the one constant in each of your relationships—you—your relationships will continue as before. What you say matters but what you do is what's critical. Ralph Waldo Emerson bluntly stated, "Who you are speaks so loudly I can't hear what you're saying." Relationships are changed by who we are within them, not merely by what we say we want them to be.

You may be in a relationship that you feel is too daunting to even try to transform it. Your particular challenging relationship may be with a parent, friend, sibling, lover, coworker, or authority figure. You may fear that if you begin to try to reshape the relationship you will lose your employment or become estranged from the other person. However, remember you are not out to remake the other person; you are out to change yourself. The other person will probably not even sense the shift at first but in time the relationship must change.

> Who you are speaks so loudly I can't hear what you're saying.
>
> —RALPH WALDO EMERSON

A relationship may seem like a huge, untamable chimera, but when you begin to embrace the cocreative nature of every relationship, you will discover that you have more power than you ever dreamed possible.

In 1999 my wife, Gail, and I were living in a small town just outside of Myrtle Beach, South Carolina. I was in a job that required me to do extensive traveling. For seven consecutive months each and every year, I left home and traveled to adjacent states. Each week I would leave on Sunday afternoon, live in a hotel room, and work until Friday morning, when I returned home. The pace was grueling but I was doing very well in my job and earning a lot of money.

Each year the first month or so apart was hardest on me and my family. The five months when I worked from home were wonderful. The time on the road was tough on us all.

In early fall, as I was concluding my final months working at home for that year, Hurricane Floyd was forming about 750 nautical miles east of the Leeward Islands. Gail and I kept checking the Weather Channel as this category four monster began to drift lazily toward the South Carolina coast.

In time hurricane trackers predicted that the storm would slam into South Carolina somewhere around Myrtle Beach. A mandatory evacuation order was issued. We boarded up our home and packed clothes for an extended stay. We loaded our cats, dogs, and goldfish into our truck, led our horses into the trailer and the entire menagerie left for the safety of the North Carolina mountains. We would wait out the storm at my mother-in-law's cabin in the Great Smokies.

Unpredictable as any hurricane, Floyd turned at the last minute and swept up the Cape Fear River into North Carolina, missing our home but flooding the South Carolina coast. We were advised not to return for a week.

We suddenly found ourselves on what might be called an "accidental vacation." We had our horses and time to be with one another. The days were unseasonably warm and the three of us rode daily up and down the mountains surrounding the cabin. Gail rode her horse and I rode mine with three-year-old Lia nestled in the front of my saddle. At night we had long leisurely dinners as a family. We reconnected in a deep way.

However, hanging like a massive, melting icicle in the back of our minds was the fact that within a few short weeks of our return home, I'd be taking off for another seven months of travel. During that 211-day period, I would be home less than 48 hours each week. This reality cast a long shadow over our good time but on the surface we were barely aware of our pending extended separation.

When the all-clear came, we loaded up our belongings and our critters and made the five-hour drive home. We had enjoyed a wonderful week together but we found ourselves sullen on the return trip.

We pulled the truck into our driveway around seven in the evening. We woke Lia, who had napped the entire trip clutching her stuffed bunny.

Gail and I unloaded our luggage and carried the saddles and other tack to the barn. Lia followed along behind us, chatting, before going into the house to play with our cat. By eight-fifteen we'd finished unloading and it was time to back the trailer into its storage space. I climbed up into the truck cab and Gail positioned herself behind the truck to help guide me.

I was tired, and inside my mind the knowledge that I would soon be leaving my family for over half a year ate at me like a cancer. This reality compounded my exhaustion, and stress began to build.

As I started backing up, I looked behind to check where Gail stood and discovered that I could not see her. Before I could soften my tone, I shouted, "Gail! Where are you?"

"I'm right here!" she shouted back, matching my tone.

"Well, I can't see you!" I said, the anger in my voice escalating. "How the hell are you supposed to help me park the trailer if I can't see you?"

"It's not my fault if you can't see me!" she barked. "I'm right here!"

"It's dark!" I screamed. "I can't see in the dark, can I? Get where I can see you, okay?"

Gail was understandably upset by my sharp tone. She, too, was tired. She, too, was grieving the fact that in a short time our family would no longer be whole and would remain that way until late spring. Gail ignored my shouts and stood quietly ignoring me.

"Gail!"

No response.

"Don't ignore me!"

Still nothing.

I *really* got mad. Without thinking, and before I knew it, I found myself out of the truck and storming toward her in a rage. Fortunately, Lia was inside playing, because for the next several minutes we shouted angrily at each other. Never before and not since have we had such a vicious argument. Back and forth we hurled mean and hurtful words peppered with expletives and threats.

Gail and I rarely, if ever, have exchanges like this. In fact, I can't remember the last time we had a disagreement that included shouting. But with the tiredness we felt, magnified by our heartache over soon being separated, we found ourselves both in a fury.

Without our knowing, Lia had stepped quietly onto the porch and was standing less than thirty feet away, hearing everything. Lia was hearing her mommy and daddy scream and curse ferociously at each other.

A moment or so later, in the midst of my hollering, I felt a gentle tug at my pants leg. I looked down to see Lia. Instantly Gail and I fell silent.

"Mommy, Daddy, can you help me?" she said.

The two of us stared down at our precious little girl silhouetted by the lights from the house.

"What?" Gail said in a restrained tone.

"Can you help me?" Lia said again.

"Help you do what?" I asked.

"There's something wrong with my coat," Lia said. "Can you fix it?"

Gail and I looked at her a moment. "What's wrong with your coat?" Gail asked, taking a step toward her. Lia extended her hands out to the side so Gail could see the coat.

"Oh, it's just inside out," Gail said gently. "Here, let me fix it." Gail pulled the jacket off, turned it right side out, and put it back on Lia. As she did, I could feel my heart beginning to slow and my blood pressure dropping.

"There you go, sweetie," Gail said.

"Thank you," Lia said. She reached up and pulled Gail down to her so she could kiss her cheek. "I love you, Mommy."

Turning to me, she reached up and grabbed my hand pulling me down so she could kiss my cheek as well. "And I love you, Daddy."

Then, without a word, she turned, ambled back into the house, and closed the door. Gail and I stood staring at each other. The anger had passed. We each took a step toward the other and embraced in a long hug.

"I love you," I said.

"And I love you," Gail responded.

I walked quietly back to the truck and started the engine, and together we parked the trailer.

Later, as I was tucking Lia into bed for the night, something occurred to me.

"Lia," I said, "you had already taken your coat off when we first got home. You were in the house playing with the cat. What made you put your coat back on?"

She turned away, clutching her stuffed bunny tightly.

"Lia," I said, "you know how to put your coat on correctly."

She ignored me.

"Look at me," I said gently.

She slowly rolled back over toward me but avoided my gaze.

"Did you put your coat on inside out deliberately and then come to ask us to help you?" I asked.

After a long moment she looked up into my eyes. "You and Mommy were saying mean things to each other. I wanted you to stop. So I did that."

"You put your coat on wrong on purpose and came out to ask our help so we'd stop fighting?" I asked.

She nodded slowly.

My eyes began to well up and I swept her up into my arms. We embraced for several minutes.

"I love you, Daddy," she said.

"I love you, too, buddy," I said. "And I love Mommy, too."

> You must not only decide that you *want* happy relationships; *you must set this as an absolute, unwavering intention* and stay the course.

Just an hour before, this toddler had witnessed two full-grown adults fighting. We were more than twice her size. How daunting must it have been for someone so small to try to change something as big as a relationship between her parents? And yet she did.

She did something herself and caused us to break the pattern of anger in which we were trapped.

Your relationship issues may seem huge; they may seem overwhelming; they may seem beyond repair; they may appear to be beyond your control. But this is not the truth. You *can* restore your relationships to health and sanity by taking the initiative to do so and following the suggestions presented in this book.

It may take some time to fully transform your connections with others, and even then there will—not *may, will*—be occasional challenges, for such is the nature of relationships. But if you have the courage and the willingness to grow and persevere, you can succeed. You must not only decide that you *want* happy relationships; *you must set this as an absolute, unwavering intention* and stay the course.

Emerson wrote, "Whatever you do, you need courage. Whatever course you decide upon, there is always someone to tell you that you are wrong. There are always difficulties arising that tempt you to believe your critics are right. To map out a course of action and follow it to an end requires some of the same courage that a soldier needs. Peace has its victories, but it takes brave men and women to win them."

Disregard those who tell you cannot succeed, look for evidence of even the smallest positive shift, and stay the course. You hold the power, right now, right where you are, to transform your connections with others into happy, healthy, and mutually supportive Complaint Free relationships.